D1300762

A giant 48-inch Northern Pike caught in Selwyn Lake, Saskatchewan.

Dave Mercer's Facts of Fishing

www.factsoffishing.com

135 Secrets Fish Don't Want You to Know

Dave Mercer

with TERRY BATTISTI

J M C P L

DISCARDED

Collins

For my family

Facts of Fishing © 2010 by Dave Mercer Outdoors Inc.
All rights reserved.

Published by Collins, an imprint of HarperCollins Publishers Ltd

First edition

No part of this book may be used or reproduced in any manner
whatsoever without the written permission of the publisher, except
in the case of brief quotations embodied in reviews.

This book has been carefully researched, and all efforts have been made
to ensure its accuracy. However, readers use at their own risk any of the
information and advice the book offers, and they should carefully study
and clearly understand the material before any such use. The authors
and publisher assume no responsibility for any injury or loss suffered
in connection with use of the book.

HarperCollins books may be purchased for educational, business,
or sales promotional use through our Special Markets Department.

HarperCollins Publishers Ltd
2 Bloor Street East, 20th Floor
Toronto, Ontario, Canada
M4W 1A8

www.harpercollins.ca

Library and Archives Canada Cataloging in Publication Data
is available upon request.

ISBN 978-1-55468-060-3

Printed and bound in the United States

Photographs © Richie Tripp/Facts of Fishing
Illustrations © Mike Del Rizzo

Introduction

Hey, everyone! Thanks for getting your copy of my *Facts of Fishing* book. To be honest, I'm still amazed someone asked me to write a book. It just goes to show you it's obviously not a prerequisite that you have to read a book before you write one. When I sat down to write this book — well, I didn't really write it, I just blabbed along and one of my good fishing buddies, Terry Battisti (a ruggedly handsome angler who drives chills of fear down the spine of any finned creature and quite frankly is a much better fisherman than me), wrote down a bunch of my thoughts.

What I wanted to accomplish with this book was to help optimize your days on the water by filling you in on some of the cool things I do with tackle and my other equipment. Some of the little tidbits of information are my own and others are tips I've learned over the years from close buddies and even some of the best professional anglers in the world — shhh, don't tell them I said that.

So obviously, you want to catch more fish or you wouldn't have bought this book. Unless, of course,

A 450-lb Grouper caught in Florida.

you just got it as a gift from your old Aunt Agnes, who didn't realize you haven't been fishing in years. Either way, thanks. This book will help you catch more fish. You may be asking yourself, "Why such a small book from such a big man?" Well, the real reason we made this book so small is so you can take it anywhere, whether it's the lake, the office, the hockey game or the crapper. Use the book as a reference or as a tool to help you experience all you want while tracking your favourite game fish. These tips will work for just about everything that swims. Remember, a fish is a fish and methods or equipment used for one will also work for others.

Thanks again and see you on the water!

P.S. If you host another fishing show or compete against me in tournaments, please don't read any further. I don't want you to know my secrets.

TIP 1:
Lifejackets

I wanted the first tip in this book to be important — something that's really going to help you. Something that no matter who you are, no matter what you fish for, no matter where you fish or even how often you fish, you will look back on and say, "Hmm, that makes sense." I started to think maybe I should tell you about some of my favourite lures. Maybe I should tell you some of my favourite little rigging tricks.

Then it came to me: Wear your lifejacket at all times! I have to be honest; this is something I haven't always done. There have been times when I've worn my jacket only when the big motor was running. But, after a scary experience that almost ended my book-writing career, I can honestly say that you will never see me on the water without a lifejacket on. Back in the day when we all had to wear those giant smelly keyhole vests, some of us might have had an excuse. But with today's super-light inflatable life-jackets, there are no excuses. So don't be a dummy — wear your personal flotation device.

TIP 2:
Green Acres Is the Place to Be

We all know fish live in weeds. And I'm no scientist so I'm not about to start a spiel on which types of weeds to fish where, because it's totally different for each species and each part of the country. One thing you can bet your boat on, though: in the fall of the year you will catch a lot more fish in green weeds. In the fall, weeds start dying off and begin turning brown. Brown weeds do not provide near as much oxygen, so the fish head for greener pastures. Look for the green weeds.

TIP 3:
Tackle Your Tackle

The funny thing about my life is there's probably only one area of it where I can say I'm truly organized, and that's my tackle. I'm not a mathematician, but I'm smart enough to figure out that the less time I waste looking for a specific lure or colour, the more time I actually get to fish. A little trick to keep things organized is simply to label all your tackle boxes. That way, when you're looking for a specific bait, it's right there. Or when you're packing for a trip, it's easy to figure out what you should or shouldn't take. Another bonus is that all those labels basically act like a menu. If the fish aren't tempted by your first or second offer, sometimes looking at your lure menu will trigger an idea that works.

TIP 4:
Pick the Right Stick

Let's face it. Rod selection is probably one of the most important aspects of successful fishing. On top of that, your rod is one of the first things your buddies see when you go fishing with them. Nobody wants to show up with a Snoopy combo and be the butt of jokes all week. If you have a cool enough rod people might not even realize how bad you suck. That being said, one of the biggest mistakes anglers make is having only one rod — especially if it's the wrong one. It's kind of like golf. Tiger Woods would never consider using a putter to drive a ball off a tee — that's why he has drivers in his bag. Enough about golf, though. I never trust a sport where water is considered a hazard. Plus those funny pants they wear make me look chubby.

One of the cool things about fishing is, although you can do it with one rod, there's no limit on how many you can carry. There's a different rod for each application — rods for crankbaits, spinnerbaits, jerkbaits, tubes, whatever the fish are biting. For the seasoned angler, rod choice is pretty simple, but for those of you just starting out, pick the highest-quality rod you can afford that can do a multitude of tasks. Something seven feet long with a medium action rated for 8- to 17-pound line. With a rod like that, you can fish a number of baits effectively and have a solid rod to begin building your arsenal.

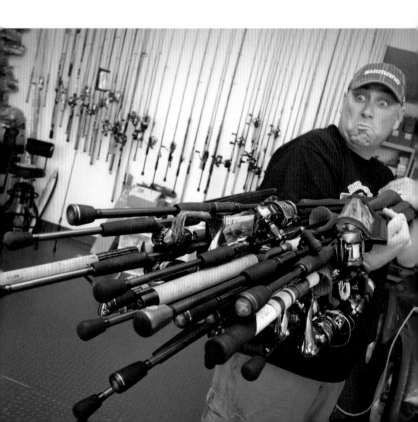

TIP 5:
The Deal with Reels

One of the most daunting tasks in fishing has to be walking into your local tackle superstore and looking down a row of what seems like miles of fishing reels. How in the world do you know what reel is right for you? Well, there are two ways to go about it. The first approach is not really proven but some people feel it works for them. Throw on a blindfold and try a game of "pin the tail on your reel." A better method, though, requires you to take off the blindfold and count bearings. Whether you are buying a spinning or casting reel, make sure it has at least four bearings. Bearings provide support to moving parts, so more bearings mean a longer life for your new reel.

TIP 6:
The Kind of Mono You Want to Get

With the changes and advances in line over the last few years, it seems like the forgotten line is nylon line — what used to be called monofilament. Believe me, I love fluorocarbon and braid, but you'll never find me in my boat without a few rods rigged with nylon line.

Just like any other tool in fishing, there's a time and a place for nylon mono. Because nylon lines float, they are best suited for use with topwater lures and with shallow-running crankbaits and jerkbaits. If that's what you're using, nylon outperforms other lines.

TIP 7:
Long-Distance Hookups

Fishing super-shallow or gin-clear waters can be one of the most heartbreaking angling experiences. I've had situations when I could see the fish moving as clearly as if they were in an aquarium or even with their backs out of the water. It seems like they'll be simple to catch — problem is if I get too close, I'll spook them. I know what you're thinking: "Not a problem, make a long cast to them."

I don't care if you can cast a full click-a-bomber (that's a Daveism for "cast a long way," folks), once you hook up with that fish, and you're using monofilament, there's going to be so much stretch in your line, you're guaranteed to lose the fish every time. I've had days where I've literally hooked dozens of fish and boated none. It's like trick-or-treating with a hole in your bag — it sucks.

The solution plain and simple: braided line. It doesn't allow you to cast any farther but what it does have is very little stretch. Because of this, your hookset will be a lot more solid and the fish will end up in your boat.

TIP 8:
Spinning Reel Setup

Incorrectly spooled line can make a great day on the water an absolute nightmare. Spending your day picking knots and twists out of your line while your buddy loads the boat isn't fun for anyone — well, except for your buddy of course. A lot of these problems can be avoided if you put your line on your reel properly.

When spooling up a spinning reel, you want the line to come off the spool in the same direction the bail is rotating. Simply lay the spool flat on the ground and wind it onto your reel. A little trick you can do to see whether you're doing it right is to put some slack in the line after you've got several feet of it on your reel. The line should lie in flat coils if it's going on properly. If you notice that your line wants to twist, flip the spool of line over and resume putting it on your reel again. Just that one little flip will eliminate the twists from your line and may end up saving your sanity.

TIP 9:
Tie One On!

When I was a kid first getting into fishing, I used to think that the simple overhand granny knot was fine. Heck, if I was fishing for really big fish, I'd just tie ten of them in a row. I guess I thought ten knots would be ten times as strong as one. I quickly learned I was wrong. So I started out on a search for the strongest knot to tie to my lures.

There are many knots to use when tying on your hook or lure. But as far as I'm concerned, there is one knot that shines over all others, and that's the Palomar Knot. This knot, tied properly, is nearly 100 percent line strength and can be used in nearly every fishing application.

How to Tie a Palomar Knot

1. Double the fishing line to form a loop. Thread the loop through the eye of the hook.
2. Make an overhand knot.
3. Pass the loop over the hook.
4. Slowly pull the two tag ends and tighten the knot.
5. Trim the tag end and you're done.

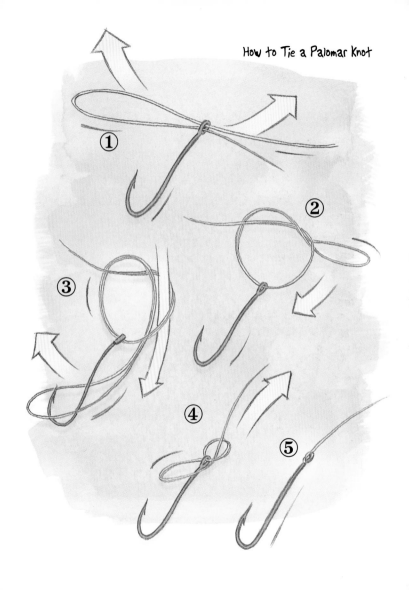

① ② ③ ④ ⑤

TIP 10:
Light-Wire Hooks

You wouldn't try driving in a railroad tie with a tack hammer, but anglers often try to do the equivalent in fishing by using light line on a light to medium-light rod while trying to drive home a heavy-wire hook.

Use light-wire hooks when fishing light line because the smaller wire diameter penetrates the fish's mouth much easier. Light-wire hooks should also be used when finesse fishing with small grubs and worms, in order to give these baits more action.

Split-Ring Swing

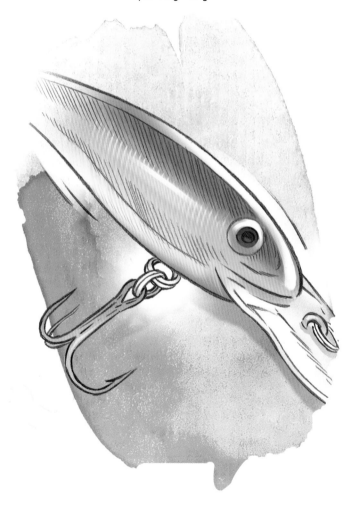

TIP 11:
Split-Ring Swing

Everybody, at one time or another, has had fish nipping at the back of their crankbait or following the bait within inches without quite committing. Here's a cool trick to help solve that problem. If you find that you're getting bit on crankbaits but the fish are hitting short or are not getting fully hooked, place an extra split ring between the hook and the original split ring. What this does is allow the hooks to swing more in the water and catch many of those short-striking fish.

TIP 12:
Trailer Hook How-To

Trailer hooks should always be used on spinner-baits. The problem is some anglers don't know the proper way to attach one. The right way to attach a trailer hook is to make sure the hook is allowed to swing freely on the bend of the main hook. You can accomplish this by first placing the trailer hook on the spinnerbait hook and then securing the trailer hook by running the spinnerbait hook through a small piece of surgical tubing or even a small piece of plastic worm. Whatever you use, just make sure the trailer hook moves freely on the spinnerbait hook. You never want to rig a trailer hook so it is locked stiff on the main hook.

How to Attach a Trailer Hook
1. Place the trailer hook onto the spinnerbait hook.
2. Slide a piece of surgical tubing or plastic worm onto the main hook to secure the trailer hook, ensuring that it can still swing freely.

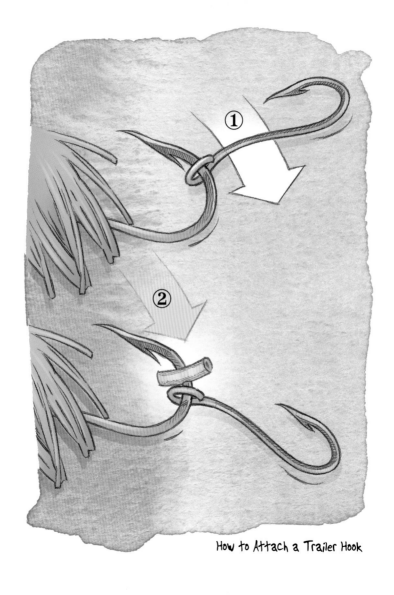

How to Attach a Trailer Hook

TIP 13:
It's Wise to Customize

Just because your lure came with a set of hooks on it doesn't mean those hooks will work for every situation. If you find you're in an area that requires heavy line due to dense cover or weeds, it's best to swap the stock hooks out to something a little bigger and stouter. On the other hand, if you're fishing with lighter than normal lines, the stock hooks may be too heavy to get a good hookset. In either case, have a selection of replacement treble hooks with you at all times so you can change hooks to meet the conditions. As a general rule, you can go up or down one hook size without altering the action of your lure.

Another little trick that has paid off for me when I have fish that follow my bait but won't commit, especially smallmouth, is a feathered treble hook at the back of the bait. It gives the lure just a little more action. I normally use white, but I hear a lot of other people use pink.

TIP 14:
In Rod We Trust

Trust me, one of the craziest things I see every year is the way people treat their fishing rods. Some people will store their rods in the bed of their pickup truck or aluminum boat and let them roll around, banging off the sides or letting their anchor(s) slide into them. Others even shut the screen door on them. Then

when their rod breaks, they blame it on the giant fish — which is generally a snag — they hooked.

Rod care is often overlooked by even the most avid angler. Why this is, I don't know. Today's rods are some of the most technologically advanced pieces of equipment out there, but they can still do you wrong if you don't pay attention to them. Take care of your rods — they're expensive and fragile. Store and transport them in rod socks or put them where they can't be banged around. This isn't just something you do during the season — you have to pay attention to them during the offseason too. When you're not using your rods, it's best to either hang them from hooks in your ceiling or place them in a rod rack so they're straight. You never want to lean them in a corner because when you come back to pick them up, you may find they're no longer straight. You always want to be able to trust your rod when a fish finally does hit. Nothing ruins a day on the water like a broken rod.

TIP 15:
Spray Is Not the Way

While this book is full of *dos*, this tip is a *don't*. ***Don't*** use spray lubes on your reels! All reels, whether they're spinning reels or casting reels, are meant to be lubricated precisely. They're just like your car — you'd never think to spray lubrication all over your ball joints or undercarriage. All this does is create a great place for dirt and grime to accumulate, which does nothing but harm your vehicle. That's why car manufacturers have strategically placed fittings in which to lube your vehicle.

Reels are the same. If you spray them with lube, you're asking to create a dirt ball, which in turn will create a reel that doesn't perform to its potential or last as long as it should. Instead, use a high-quality reel lube that comes in a squeeze bottle. This way you can get the lube exactly where it needs to go. So here's a do: get into the habit of lubing your reels in the offseason — that way you're guaranteed to do it at least once a year. It's also a great way to pass the cold winter months. Set up your reel service station in front of your television, pop in your favourite movie or, hey, if you can't think of anything else to watch, just turn on *Facts of Fishing*.

TIP 16:
Layin' It on the Line

I am an absolute competitive-fishing freak. I love going out with a buddy and watching him catch fish, but I don't like it when he catches more than I do. Sometimes it's the most subtle thing that can make the difference.

Here's a good example. On one fishing trip I got absolutely whupped on by one of my fishing buddies, who will remain nameless because he beat me that day and doesn't deserve to be in my book. We were throwing crankbaits for staging salmon. You want to talk about a blast — hook into a thirty-plus-pound Chinook with a crankbait and it's game on.

Anyway, we headed out early one morning and the fish were on fire for this guy. The problem was, they weren't even smouldering for me. I watched him catch one Chinook after another, and I changed everything to match his setup. I changed my bait to the exact bait he was using; I changed my retrieve speed to match his; I changed the area where I was casting, the distance — everything — all to match what he was doing. At one point, when he was taking a break after wrestling so many fish into the boat, I actually cut the bait off his line and tried my luck — still nothing.

The problem? Well, I'd just cut the problem — it was the line. I was using a heavier-test line than he was, so his bait was getting deeper. That day I learned a valuable lesson: line can play a huge role in the depth your bait dives.

Heavy line will make a lure run shallower and light line will allow your bait to get down deeper.

TIP 17:
How to Get Snags Out

Knowing how to get a snag out will not only save you a whack of money — it will also make you a better angler. The reason for this is you'll have the confidence to fish in the cover, which is where fish live.

When you do get a snag, the important thing to remember is to avoid making your life more difficult. When you feel your lure hang, don't start pulling and tugging. That's only going to drive your hooks deeper in the snag and make it more difficult to get out.

At some point you're going to have to get your lure back, and one of the easiest techniques is known as the Bow and Arrow. Rear your rod back, just keeping the line taut. Then grab the line between your reel and your first guide and pull it away from the rod with your free hand. Once you have good tension in the rod and line, fling the rod forward and release the line from your hand at the same time. This action will create a wave in the line that will push the bait away from the snag.

If that doesn't work, don't worry, you're not busted yet. The next thing to try is looking at the problem from another angle. Just move your position to the other side of the snag. You'd be amazed how quickly you can pull out of a snag by changing the angle of the line. It's a lot like getting in a car wreck. If you go out in a parking lot and drive into someone's car, most of us wouldn't try to keep driving through it. All you have to do is back away and you're out. Unfortunately, that's not what most anglers try to do when they get snagged.

TIP 18:
Keep It Low

When fishing a jig or any bottom-contact bait in the wind, detecting a strike can be difficult. One of the easiest ways to deal with this is to keep your rod tip low to the water. With most fishing situations, you want to fish a high rod because you have more sensitivity that way. Not if the wind is blowing, though. The reason for this is your line will be blown into a huge bow and the only thing you'll feel taking your bait is a sperm whale. Keep your rod tip and line close to the surface and you'll be amazed how much more you'll feel on those windy days.

TIP 19:
What's My Line?

Go to any tackle shop and there are literally hundreds of different types of line — each one claiming to be better than another in some way. Some are stronger, some cast longer, some are limper and some are stiffer. How's an angler to figure out what characteristics are right for the situation?

Every line has its time and every technique has a preferred line. So you may end up using every one of those lines at one point or another. But the general rule for choosing among them is pretty simple. When using a spinning reel, pick a limper line with little or no memory. This will allow the line to flow off the reel with ease and will decrease the chances of birds' nests or loops forming on the spool.

On the other hand, when using casting gear, use a line that has better abrasion resistance. This generally means a stiffer line, but because of the way the line comes off a casting reel, stiffer line won't be a problem.

TIP 20:
The Reel Knot

Many anglers have problems attaching line to their reels. This is because it's difficult to cinch a knot down below the lip of the spool. But here's a knot that you actually cinch before it gets down to the spool — it's called the San Diego Jam Knot (see page 34). It's also great to use when you're using fluorocarbon lines (see page 35).

How to Tie a San Diego Jam Knot (for a reel)
1. Wrap the line around the reel and double it back. Take the tag end of the line and wrap it back over itself and the standing line six times.
2. Thread the tag end through the open loop at the top of the knot and tighten.

How to Tie a San Diego Jam Knot (for a fishing hook)
1. Thread the line through the eye of the hook and double it back.
2. Take the tag end of the line and wrap it back over itself and the standing line six times.
3. Pass the tag end through the open loop.
4. Tighten.

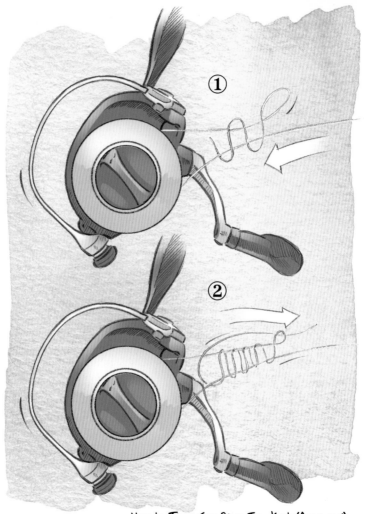

How to Tie a San Diego Jam Knot (for a reel)

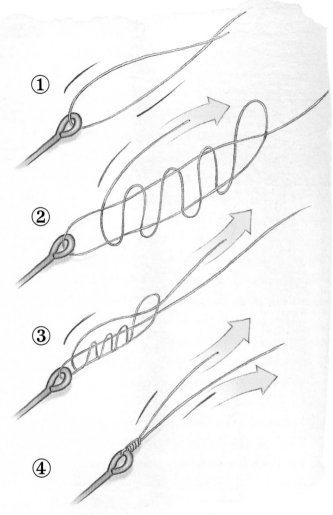

① ② ③ ④

How to Tie a San Diego Jam Knot (for a fishing hook)

TIP 21:
Feel It in Your Finger

With today's ultra-sensitive rods and braided lines you can feel a fish fart underwater. Even with these improvements, though, I still don't want to miss a fish. Maybe it's my tournament background or my ultra-competitive nature. In any event, you can't count on technology to do all your work for you. A quick trick to help turn the odds in your favour is to simply rest the line on your forefinger as you work your bait back to the boat. This gives you one more point of contact with your finned foe. You'll feel any subtle difference in the movement of the line, which is quite often a fish that might otherwise have got away.

TIP 22:
Sharpen Up

It's been said that I'm not the sharpest knife in the drawer. But one thing I do believe in is sharp hooks. Today's hooks rarely need to be sharpened when they come out of the pack, but you may find your hook becomes dull as you use it, and a dull hook is about as useful as a dull knife. In order to sharpen hooks properly, buy yourself a good metal hook file. (Sharpening stones are no good because they wear fast and grooves form on their surfaces.) Make sure you score the hook from only one direction and at an angle that is nearly flush with the wire to avoid grinding off the tip.

TIP 23:
Worm Weights

I've got to tell you, until I started writing this book I had no idea how much different fishing crap there is out there. I mean, I own all this stuff but I've never actually sat down and listed it. I sure hope my wife doesn't pick up this book and realize just how much money I've been spending all these years.

Just like anything else, there's a bunch of different styles of weights to match different fishing situations. One of the most popular is a worm weight. Standard cone-shaped worm weights are great for Texas-rigged plastic baits, but they're also great for finesse Carolina rigs. Their cone shape comes through rocks and vegetation with ease. Novice anglers are often confused about these weights due to their name — worm weights. But these little bullet-shaped weights aren't just designed to fish worms. They're perfect for just about any soft plastic bait you want to slide through cover.

TIP 24:
Bobber-Stop Security

Okay, here's another example of a simple piece of fishing equipment designed for one thing and being used for something entirely different. MacGyver has nothing on us anglers. Seems we can find a use for anything.

A bobber stop is a very versatile piece of equipment. Not only can it be used to dangle bait at a specific depth below a bobber, it can be used to help prevent knot damage on Carolina and Texas rigs. To use the bobber stop for knot protection, place the stop on the line after you thread on your sliding sinker. Then tie the swivel or hook on and run the bobber stop down to the knot. Now the sinker can't harm the knot.

Protecting a Knot with a Bobber Stop

TIP 25:
Crack Kills

No, not that type of crack. The type of crack I want to warn against, while not as deadly, will kill your opportunity to catch a giant fish. I'm talking about a crack anywhere on any of your line guides. The whole idea of a line guide is to protect your line as you reel your lure back to the boat or fight a fish. The exact opposite can happen if you don't pay attention to them. Line guides develop microscopic cracks that can wear line down or even break it on a hookset. One way to check for these cracks is to run a piece of cotton ball through the guide. If a guide has a crack, the cotton will hang up in it. If your cotton ball snags, send the rod to a repair shop and have the guide replaced.

Dave's FISHING TALES

It Can Happen to Anyone

There are two kinds of thoughts about weddings — one from a woman's point of view and the other from a man's. That would be fine, since men and women think differently regarding just about everything, except in this case the two perspectives are about as far apart as you can get. For example, girls are told from the earliest of ages that one day they'll grow up and meet this amazing Prince Charming fellow who will propose to them. Then they'll have this wonderful day where everybody dotes on them and tells them how beautiful they look and they'll live happily ever after.

On the other hand, we guys are told from the time we're five years old — by just about every male member of society — not to get married. For men, a wedding is an evil, horrible day when we're made to dress up in penguin suits and forced to acknowledge that afterwards we'll have to live with this new person called a "wife," who will never let us go fishing (and will force us to put down the toilet seat and otherwise totally destroy our lives). No wonder guys fear weddings — we're taught to.

I'm pretty lucky, though. My wife does none of the things I was warned she would, and I really enjoyed my wedding — especially the honeymoon. Now get your mind out of the gutter, that's not what I'm talking about. You see, I always told my wife that one of the things I wanted to do on our honeymoon was go fishing. So, when we booked our honeymoon I really didn't care where we went, as long as I could fish.

The wedding went off without a hitch and we headed to Mexico shortly after to celebrate. After we arrived, my wife, being the special girl that she is, snuck down to the beach and booked us a fishing charter.

When she came back she showed me a picture from the charter service. The picture was of a 40-foot boat fully decked out with top-of-the-line offshore rods and reels, and loaded with gorgeous models and giant fish. I mean, this was one step short of a beer commercial — I couldn't believe it! The next morning I'd be heading out, fishing on my honeymoon as I had always dreamed. I could see the headline: "Angler catches new world record sailfish while on honeymoon!" Let me tell you — I was excited!

The next morning I woke up, walked down to the dock and realized I'd been dreaming in more ways than one. Yes, my bride really had chartered us a day on the water. But what I quickly learned is sometimes the postcard picture isn't exactly an accurate depiction of reality. The charter company didn't lie about the 40-foot boat — they just didn't mention it was only four feet wide. I thought, "Okay, no big deal. I'll go fishing in the floating banana." But that wasn't the last disappointment.

Once we boarded, it didn't take long for me to notice the water in the bottom of the boat. Not wanting to ruin the day, I reassured myself with the thought that I'm a good swimmer, and Captain Felipe assured my bride and me that everything would be fine. With that, we pushed off from the dock and headed out fishing.

Away from the dock, my confidence in the situation didn't improve. It wasn't long before I noticed that although the banana boat had two motors, only one of them worked — the other just seemed to billow smoke like the dry-ice machine at your local nightclub. But again, rationalization took over and I started thinking; "Hey, I'm in Mexico doing something that every guy told me I wouldn't do! They'd all told me that once you get married you're not allowed to fish anymore. I mean, sure the boat's only four feet wide, it's filling with water and has only one working engine, but I'm fishing and that's what life is all about." Nothing was going to ruin this good time with my beautiful new wife. Or so I thought . . .

About an hour into our trip, the wind started to pick up pretty hard. I'm not sure how much time you've spent in a four-foot-wide boat, but I can tell you they're not designed for rough water. Needless to say, the boat was rolling hard and the wind wasn't doing me any favours by blowing every last puff of diesel exhaust in my direction. Sure, it wasn't perfect, and I did begin to feel an unfamiliar stirring in my stomach, but hey, I was fishing.

Twenty minutes after the wind picked up, that unfamiliar stirring in my stomach had climbed its way up to my throat. Beads of sweat were streaming down my brow — it took every ounce of strength I had to hold in the fajitas I'd eaten for dinner the night before. "Could this be happening to me?" I asked. "Could I be getting seasick?"

One thing I know about getting seasick is that once you start asking yourself if it's happening, it's happening. I put up a valiant battle, but before I knew it I was hanging off the side of the boat in a cloud of diesel exhaust, and what a short time earlier had been my honeymoon fishing trip had become my very own personal puke party!

In light of all that, Captain Felipe was a good captain. He knew one of the best things to do in a situation like this was to get my mind off my retching stomach. In order to do this, he started firing questions at me so I'd have to think about something other than liberating the restless fajitas in my gut. He started out asking, "Señor Dave, where are you from?"

"UGHAAA — Canada," I answered.

"Señor Dave, what part of Canada?" was his next query.

"UGHAAA — Toronto."

"Señor Dave, that's the home of my favourite baseball team — the Toronto Blue Jays. Do you like them?"

"UGHAAA — yes."

Then came one of the worst questions I've ever been asked in my life, and I'm sure, to this day, there's a fishing guide in Mexico that thinks I'm an absolute liar.

"Señor Dave, what do you do for a living?"

I turned away from the heaving waves and the spectacle of the small fish feeding off my chum, looked at him straight in the eyes and said, "UGHAAAA — I'm a professional fisherman."

I've been to Cinco de Mayo and many other Mexican celebrations, and I can honestly tell you that I have never, ever heard a Mexican laugh as loud as Captain Felipe did that day.

TIP 26:
Keep Your Cork Clean

Hey, you know how your mom used to tell you to change your underwear because you didn't want to get in an accident with dirty underwear? That never made sense to me because I'm pretty sure if I'm in an accident I'm going to crap my pants anyway. But what does make sense to me is the need to keep the cork on your rod clean. Cork grips, after a hard year of use, become soiled and can eventually become slick. In order to keep your cork grips clean, take some Comet and sprinkle it on a moist sponge and scrub the dirt off the grip. Then rinse thoroughly with water and dry. After the grip has completely dried, apply some wood spray wax to the cork. The wax seals the cork and keeps it from deteriorating. Of course, clean underwear is still a good idea. It just won't help you catch fish.

TIP 27:
Long Shot

I would say that 90 percent of the time I'm fishing a drop shot, my bait is generally 12 to 18 inches off the bottom. But you never know ahead of time how far off the bottom you're going to want to end up, and finding the right depth can seem like a bit of a chore. A little trick I began using is to start off with a long tag end. This allows me to determine how far off the bottom the fish want the bait. After all, it's a lot easier to make the tag shorter than it is to make it longer. Normally I'll start with a two- to three-foot tag end, unless I see on the graph that the fish are six feet off the bottom, and place the sinker at the end of the tag. From there I can adjust the sinker up until I find out how far up the fish want the bait. By doing it this way, I don't have to retie the rig if the fish want the bait high in the water column.

This 6 1/2-lb Smallie fell for the long shot.

TIP 28:
Close Your Eyes

So I'm out on the water and I'm dunking deep weeds with a Texas-rigged worm. I feel the familiar tap of a fish biting. I rear back, set the hook and end up with nothing but line.

Initially I thought I'd broken my line, but when I went to retie I realized the knot was still there. "Huh, must have broken the hook," I thought. Well, it happened a couple more times before I got smart. I wasn't breaking the hook or line. I just needed to learn to close my eyes.

A lot of hooks come from the factory with a small gap at the hook eye. This isn't much of a problem when using nylon monofilament line or fluorocarbon but it can spell disaster when using braided line. When using braid, make sure you close this gap by crimping it shut with a pair of pliers. If you don't, you run the risk of the line slipping into the gap and coming away from the hook. It may not happen every time, mind you. But when you get that personal-best fish on, that's when it will happen.

TIP 29:
Stay Smelly

Most anglers will agree that scents make sense when you're fishing. The problem with scents is they wear off the bait quickly and have to be reapplied. One cool thing about tube baits is that they are hollow and can be filled with anything you jam up them. One of the things I like to put up my tubes is a cotton ball saturated with scent. The cotton ball will stay in the tube and slowly release scent.

TIP 30:
Go Finger

One of the perceived drawbacks of a spinning reel is that it seems less accurate than a casting reel simply because you're not in constant contact with the line. For example, with a casting reel, if I want to stop a bait over a stump, the edge of a weedline or any type of fish-holding cover, all I have to do is apply pressure to the spool with my thumb and I can stop the lure in mid-air right over the target. Well, nearly the same can be done with a spinning reel, though unfortunately most anglers just flip the bail, fire their bait out and basically pray for accuracy.

Something that will really benefit your accuracy is to feather the line with your forefinger as your lure heads to the target. Also, using your forefinger to pick up the line after a cast is one good way to make sure that those nasty loops don't develop on the spool of your reel.

TIP 31:
Fear the Fray

Over the last number of years a lot of the lakes in the north have been overrun by zebra mussels. While these little critters may seem harmless to some, they create havoc for anglers. A mussel bed on the bottom of your lake or mussels stuck to a dock piling might as well be a bouquet of razor blades — these things will cut through your line in a heartbeat. And many anglers just end up getting into more trouble as they try to zebra-proof their line. A lot of people try to combat the invasive mussels by spooling up their reel with some heavy braided line, thinking there's no way the little creatures are going to cut through 50-pound test.

What they fail to realize is that 50-pound test is 50 pounds of pulling force. In this case, you don't need strength as much as you need abrasion resistance. And, for abrasion resistance, you actually want a good fluorocarbon. Fluorocarbon lines offer more abrasion resistance than nylon or even braided lines. They're not going to save the world from zebra mussels, but they should at least get your bait back to the boat.

TIP 32:
Beware of Degreasers

I love WD-40, but never use it on your reels unless you are cleaning them. Products like WD-40 are actually degreasers and will do more harm than good. If you want your reel to last a lifetime, use only a high-quality reel lube.

TIP 33:
Line to Line

One thing I know a lot about is knots. No, I didn't get a badge in Cub Scouts — I just tested a whole bunch of knots over the years. It's not hard to tell if you have a good knot or a bad knot. And believe me, I had lots of bad ones. One of the knots that scares most anglers is tying line to line.

There are a number of line-to-line knots, but the one I use all the time is the Double Uni Knot. Use this for tying fluorocarbon to fluorocarbon or nylon to nylon. When it comes to tying nylon or fluorocarbon to braided lines, this is the knot to use.

How to Tie a Double Uni Knot
1. Place the two lines parallel to each other. Beginning with either line, form a circle with both "legs" on the same side of the second line. Take one leg and turn it through the circle and over the standing line five times. Slowly pull the tag end while holding the other, making sure the barrels do not jump over one another. Pull the knot tight.
2. Repeat the same process with the second line.
3. Once the two Uni Knots are created, pull the two standing lines.
4. The Uni Knots should butt up against one another.

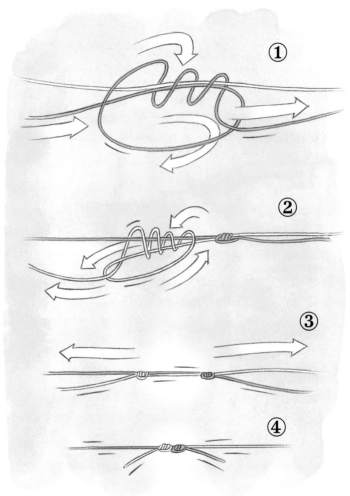

① ② ③ ④

How to Tie a Double Uni Knot

TIP 34:
Shrink Tube Savings

I once met an old guy at a tournament. He spent a bunch of time asking me how much my boat cost, how much gas I burnt, how many lures I used and how many fish I caught. After a quick calculation he shook his head in disbelief and asked me why I do what I do. According to him, my fish worked out to be several thousands of dollars per pound. Yes, this sport can definitely cost a lot. So any tip I can give you that will save you money will go a long way. Here's a trick that will help you conserve those expensive plastics.

Many hooks today don't come with keeper barbs on them. Or, if they do, they're too small to actually work. You can add your own keeper to a hook by using a small piece of shrink tubing. Cut one end at a 45-degree angle and then run it onto the hook — angled end towards the eye. Now heat the tubing with a candle until the tubing is tight on the hook. As the tubing cools, squeeze the angled end away from the hook shaft so it forms a nice barb. This little tip will keep your soft plastic baits on your hook, and a bit of money safely in your wallet.

TIP 35:
Get the Drop on Them

Drop-shotting is one of those weird techniques that seems to get a bad rap for being really technical. If you really look at it, though, it's pretty simple. And if you're fishing for smallmouths on the Great Lakes, drop-shotting is a staple. My favourite drop-shot sinkers are the long cylindrical type, since they come through rock vegetation and zebra mussels with ease. The other thing I like about these sinkers is their quick-connect clips. That's one less knot to tie. And if one of these sinkers does get hung up, I can pull the line through the clip and get my hook and bait back.

TIP 36:
Oval — The New Round

Somebody once told me you can't reinvent the wheel. Man, oh man, were they ever wrong. One example of a successful reinvention is the oval split ring — a little piece of equipment I find myself using more and more. Have you ever found that while using split rings it's difficult to keep the knot from moving into the split area of the ring? This is a problem because the sharp edges of the split can weaken your knot and cause a great deal of pain when that fish of a lifetime says bye-bye as your line breaks. One way to alleviate this problem is to use oval split rings. On oval split rings, the split is on the side of the ring well away from where your knot is. And because the ring is oval, your knot has no chance of sliding down into the split.

TIP 37:
Beads Are for Mardi Gras

While glass beads and plastic beads and all these different sound-making, light-reflecting devices seem to make sense, in my years of experience beads just don't do much good. I don't care if you're throwing a C-rig, a worm harness or a drop shot — other than for Mardi Gras, beads have no value. That being said, it's unbelievable the value they have at Mardi Gras.

TIP 38:
Do Scents Make Sense?

There's a lot of controversy as to whether or not scents actually attract fish. Here's what I know. Large predatory fish, like muskie and pike, like to eat other smaller fish. While I'm not a fish or a scientist, I have to believe these prey don't like to get eaten. So if I happen to hook into one of these freshwater barracuda, I make sure to apply scent not just to my bait but also to myself — I wash my hands with it to mask the scent of the predator fish. I've seen it happen enough times to know that bass don't like the smell of the fish that eat them. I would be going along catching bass after bass and then hook a muskie — and the bite would stop. Only after I'd washed the muskie scent off my hands and the lure and reapplied an attractive scent would the bite pick back up.

Another thing I know about scent is — and again, I'm not a fish — Irish Spring, Aqua Velva, gas and all sorts of other things we touch on a daily basis don't smell natural to fish. So whether fish scent attracts fish or not, it definitely masks the scents that deter them.

TIP 39:
Back Off Your Drags

One of the most important features of your reel is the drag. That's because it keeps you from losing fish. If you choose to hit the water with a reel that has a jumpy drag and more hiccups than Otis the Drunk from *The Andy Griffith Show*, you're not doing yourself any favours.

At the end of your season, what you need to do to extend the life of your reels is to back their drags off. For casting reels, the best way to do this is to back off the star drag all the way, hold the spool with your thumb and turn the reel handle. With a spinning reel, back the drag off and turn the spool. In both cases what this does is separate the fibre washers from the metal washers in the drag system. If you leave them clamped down for months at a time, the soft fibre washers will stick to the metal washers in your reel and your drag will forever be jerky.

Amazon River Peacock Bass

TIP 40:
The Finger Flip

Some call them wind knots or loose line. I call them a $&!!%# disaster! Far too often I hear people blame cheap line, bad reels or the way they put their line on their reel as the reason for this disaster when, in most cases, it's the automatic bail trip that creates slack in the line at the spool. Always flip your bail manually. It seems easier to just turn the handle and use the auto feature, but by manually flipping the bail, you can decrease the number of loops that form and, therefore, decrease the frequency of those nasty tangles of line that come off your reel, which can take a lot of time to undo.

TIP 41:
Top Knot

When considering knots, most anglers just think of strength or how easy the knot is to tie. But some knots can actually help you catch fish by allowing the bait to have better action. The loop knot is one of these. Although this knot isn't as strong as the Palomar Knot, it allows the bait to swing freely, which gives your topwater lure more action.

How to Tie a Loop Knot

1. Tie an overhand knot, leaving at least 5" of line at the tag end. Do not tighten the knot. Run the end through the eyelet in the lure.
2. Thread the end back through the overhand knot.
3. Wrap the end around the line three times.
4. Thread the end through the back of the overhand knot.
5. Pass the end through the loop.
6. Tighten.

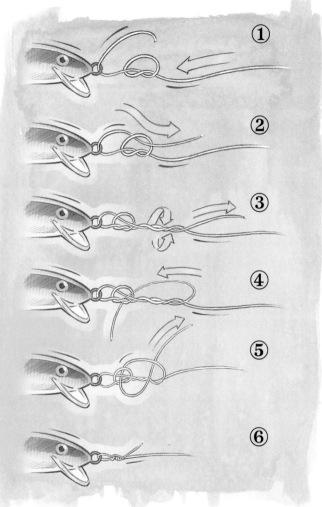

① ② ③ ④ ⑤ ⑥

How to Tie a Loop Knot

TIP 42:
That Sinking Feeling

There have been times in the past when my girl-friends have accused me of not being sensitive. I'm here to tell you, they're totally wrong. I've even cried several times after losing a fish. But enough about me. The one sensitive thing you want on your boat is your line. One of the great attributes of fluorocarbon is its sensitivity.

Many people say that fluorocarbon lines are more sensitive because they don't stretch — this isn't the case at all. In fact, fluorocarbon lines stretch just as much as nylon lines. So then, why is fluorocarbon line more sensitive if it stretches as much as nylon? Well, the answer is, it sinks. Because of that property, you have less slack between you and your lure.

Also, because fluorocarbon line sinks, you can use it to help keep your lure in a specific part of the water column. Much like nylon lines can keep your bait higher in the water, you can use fluorocarbon to make your bait go deeper. Sensitive and deep — if only those ex-girlfriends could see me now.

TIP 43:
Handful of Heartache

I don't know why, but one thing I can count on about fishing is if you're shooting a show or competing in a tournament, freaky stuff just happens. It seems the more money there is on the line, or the bigger the tournament, the crazier the things that happen.

I first learned about this phenomenon during one of the first tournaments I actually had a chance to win. On the final day I broke off a dozen fish, and believe me, you think you hate losing fish, imagine losing a fish that could cost you several thousand dollars.

While that kind of money means a lot to anybody, at the time it meant even more to me. Back then I was driving a pickup I used to call the Fred Flintstone truck. Why? Because, just like Fred's ride, my truck actually had a hole in the driver's side floor that I could stick my feet through. Thank God for floor mats or my mom would never have let me leave the house in that clunker. In any case, I was ready for a new vehicle, and losing one fish after another was not going to help me at all.

"Maybe it's bad line," I thought, so I swapped it out for something else. That didn't help, and I lost a couple more.

"Maybe it isn't heavy enough," I fretted, and went to a stronger line. That didn't help either. After I lost a few more I started to check the guides on my rod to see if there was a chip in them. Nothing.

I continued to lose fish and then fell to the bottom of the boat in the fetal position, sobbing to myself and wondering why this had happened to me. If I'd only known, the problem was in my hand all along. I had a crack in the levelwind of my reel.

Always check the levelwind on your casting reels and the line roller on your spinning reels to make sure they are in good working order. Most good-quality casting reels these days have silicon carbide line guides. Although they are a hard material, they can crack and lead to line breakage. On your spinning reels, make sure the line roller is moving freely and is also free of nicks or scratches. Otherwise you might find yourself weeping on the floor of your boat.

TIP 44:
Performance-Enhanced Line

Have you ever had a spot that you just knew had a fish in it but there was no possible way you'd get it out? I grew up on a lake called Scugog, otherwise known as The Bog. This is a weed-infested, stump-riddled mud hole that is absolutely jam-packed with fish. I remember parts of the lake that were so choked with lily pads, arrowheads and just about any other weed you can think of, it was nearly impossible to get a fish out. Back then we just thought that was the way it was. You're going to hook a bunch, lose a bunch and hopefully end up with a few of the right ones by the time it was all done.

Then along came braided line. This stuff totally changed the game. Where braid shines is when you're fishing in heavy cover like stumps, heavy weeds, lily pads or dock situations. Braid also shines in topwater applications, especially when fishing frogs, because it floats.

TIP 45:
Split Shot

Definitely the most common weight known to man is the split shot. It's usually the first weight any of us ever used. But for some strange reason, as anglers advance in ability, many of them forget about the split shot.

Here's a tip for those who use a lot of split shot: when buying split shot, choose the ones that are completely round. Yes, the ones with ears are much easier to deal with in that you can take them off at will. But those little ears have a tendency to get caught on rocks and especially vegetation. No, you won't be able to take the round split shots off, but if you need to take them off, it's probably time to retie your hook again anyway.

TIP 46:
Heavy-Wire Hooks

Imagine how weird it would seem if a tow truck driver showed up to pull you out of a ditch with his brand-new souped-up high-power tow truck and then pulled out a coat hanger to hook up to your car. That's exactly what happens on the water on a daily basis.

In instances where you find yourself around thick cover using lines heavier than 12-pound test, heavy-gauge wire hooks are a must. Don't get caught fishing a light-wire hook in these instances, because sooner or later you're going to set the hook on that monster bass, your light-wire hook is going to open up and all you'll have in your hand is a straight piece of wire — its tip pointing in the direction of your fish as it swims away.

TIP 47:
Swivels

All right, this tip isn't going to be popular with the swivel manufacturers, but I've got to say it: there is only one good use of swivels and that's as a leader connection. Swivels should never be attached to any lure or hook except a herring dodger used in trolling. I sure hope the swivel mafia isn't after me now.

TIP 48:
Them's the Brakes

Back when I was thirteen, I got a chance to fish with one of my angling idols, Rocky Crawford. I mean, this dude had just won the Canadian Classic. Girls dream of going on dates with the three Jonas Brothers; little fishing freaks like me dreamed of a day on the water with Rocky Crawford.

I figured this was going to be my opportunity to show off my fishing skills to a real pro angler. I wanted to be ready. The one weak point in my arsenal at that point was baitcasting reels — I hadn't become proficient with them yet. But that wasn't a problem, since all I had to do was practise.

Before the trip, I spent hours in the driveway in front of my house practising my casting, and accomplished two things. First, I confirmed my neighbours' belief that I was one of the weirdest kids on the street. Second, I became pretty good with a baitcasting reel.

Well, the big day came and I stepped up to the front deck of the boat right beside one of my idols. I picked up my baitcaster and the feeling I had at that moment can't be much different than what a rookie feels the first time he steps up to the plate at Yankee Stadium.

I reared back with my rod and fired a cast that I'd envisioned sailing out into the lake for miles. Unfortunately, that cast came to a screeching halt and landed literally six feet from the boat. While I quickly picked that backlash out, I looked out of the corner of my eye at Rocky as he pretended not to notice. I wrote my failure off to nerves and wound up for cast number two. Well, casts two, three, four, five, six, seven and eight all had the exact same result. It was like a backlash-a-palooza. I couldn't believe this was happening to me. So I put my bait-caster away, picked up a spinning rod and fished the day away.

After that dreadful experience, I realized that I had made a huge mistake all those days I'd prac-tised in the driveway. I had always cast with the wind, but you don't always have that option when you're out on the water. In my defence, things were a lot tougher back then. The baitcasting reels of my youth didn't have the intricate braking systems available on today's models.

Today's reels can beat just about any backlash by using the casting brakes located opposite of the spool tension knob. When the spool spins, these brakes rub against a raceway and slow the spool down by friction. The brakes affect the spool speed on the entire cast, but have their greatest effect at the beginning. This quality makes them great for tuning your reel when casting into the wind. These brakes can be found under the sideplate and ride on small pins located on the spool. On most modern reels, there are four to six brakes that can be activated by pulling them away from the spool shaft until they click. The more brakes you activate, the faster the spool will slow down, giving you more control over your cast. If only I'd had one of those when I was a kid.

TIP 49:
Casting Reel

I've met some anglers who swear the only useful thing they've done with a baitcaster is raise the stock of line companies by going through shelves of new line because of continuous backlashes. If they only put their line on correctly from the get-go, they'd have far fewer problems. To spool a casting reel the correct way, simply place a pencil through the spool, have a friend hold the pencil so line comes off the top of the spool and wind it on your reel. Also, don't forget to keep pressure on the new line spool so the fresh line is packed tightly on your reel.

TIP 50:
Rough Up Your Bait

I don't know about you, but I find salted tubes work way better than unsalted tubes. But a funny thing I have noticed over the years is that salted tubes work better after they've caught a few fish. I think this is because the salt in the plastic is released as the tube gets roughed up by the fish. So, in order to make my salted tubes more productive right out of the package, I squeeze them with my fingers and roll them between my hands to release their salt. Now I don't have to wait for a fish to do it for me.

Killed by My Kill Switch

Years ago, when I first started tournament fishing, I was freakishly jacked up come the dawn of tournament morning. I'd have my tunes cranked at the boat ramp, thinking, "Everybody on the water better look out because I'm going fishing!" I probably looked more like an NFL player with 'roid-rage than a tournament angler. Since then I've mellowed quite a bit, but back in those days it was a whole different story — and it all had to do with how the tournaments start.

Most tournaments are kicked off with what is called "blastoff." All 150 competitors line up with their high-performance bass boats in preparation to race down the lake at 75 miles per hour to their chosen hotspots. During these times, there's enough horsepower and testosterone floating in the area to make even Tim "The Tool Man" Taylor nervous. While professional anglers rarely agree with each other on anything, there's one thing we all agree on: the feeling you get while sitting on a quiet lake surrounded by 149 other pros in high-performance boats with engines rumbling and the clock ticking down to blastoff is awesome.

One feeling that is not so awesome, though, is being literally sixty seconds from your blastoff time and hearing a high-performance engine stop rumbling — particularly if it's your engine. If you're a high-strung, hyped-up teenager who feels his only shot at fishing superstardom just shut down with his engine, matters are even worse. Well, that's what happened to me.

Before I go into the rest of that story though, let me tell you a little about myself that you probably don't know. I am officially the world's least handy man alive — there are probably some dead men that are handier than me. I can't fix anything. I failed auto shop for crying out loud! There are some people in this world who will tell you they're not very handy at all — don't take them seriously until you've compared them to me. I can't even change a tire. It's not that I'm lazy. I just have no idea how to do it.

Anyway, back to the story.

When my engine stopped during that testoster-one-filled moment, sixty seconds before the blast-off, I did the only thing somebody in my situation could do. I dug deep into my ultra-competitive core and in the loudest, shrillest voice that has ever resonated through my vocal cords, I screamed, "HEEEEELLLPPPPP!"

Luckily, some tournaments have support teams to help the competitors in the event they have mechanical troubles. Naturally, due to my inability to fix anything, I'd quickly become friends with these guys before the tournament and when they heard my screams, they jumped into their boat and raced towards my lifeless vessel.

Once they reached me, they jumped onto the back deck, removed the engine cowling, lifted the maintenance hatch and began twisting, tightening, pumping and adjusting everything they thought could have caused the problem. After each new adjustment, they'd yell towards me, "Try it!" and I would turn the key.

Nothing.

More adjustments.

"Try it now!"

Nothing.

"Try it again!"

Still nothing.

Although they were perplexed, they didn't quit. They knew how much this tournament meant to me and I'm sure they could see the heartbreak in my eyes as my competition raced off to fish.

There wasn't much more for me to do but look down towards the bottom of my boat in defeat, muttering to myself and wondering how this could have been happening to me. That's when I saw it — something that filled me with joy and horror all at the same time. My kill switch.

Most boats come equipped with a small switch that attaches the ignition to the boat driver. In the event the driver gets thrown from the boat, the switch is pulled and kills the engine.

On the other hand, if the switch isn't connected, your motor won't start.

Somehow, in my panic to fish that day, I'd unknowingly pulled my kill switch and cried for help. So there I was sitting, the solution in my hands, as the top-notch mechanics rifled through every part of my boat searching for the answer. Obviously, they figured that a professional fisherman would have thought to check his kill switch before screaming like a helpless kid who just lost his helium-filled balloon at the carnival.

The funny thing was I wasn't humiliated by my screaming, my inability to fix things or my uncontrolled panic. But after all the time they'd spent trying to find the problem, I wasn't about to tell them I had found it — that would be too humiliating. So I discreetly reconnected the kill switch and waited for them to ask me to try to start the engine again. Once they did, the motor fired to life, just as I knew it would, and I sped off to battle the bass.

I often wonder what the mechanics thought the problem was that day. I ran into one of them one day and he told me it must have been a loose wire or nut. If he only knew how right he was!

TIP 51:
Keep Your Pants Up

Don't you hate getting your pants pulled down? Well, it's something that happens all the time when you're fishing a grub and jighead. Don't worry, it's not somebody actually pulling down your pants — it's just a term anglers use to describe a small fish pulling a grub down the shank of your hook. When that grub is pulled down, it doesn't look natural, and your chances of a fish eating it decrease drastically. So here's what you want to do: simply add a dab of superglue to the collar of the jig and slide the grub over the glue. This will prevent your grub, or pants as we say, from being pulled down the shank of the hook.

TIP 52:
Get Wacky

This next tip just goes to show you that things don't have to look good to us to look good to a fish. When I first saw the "wacky" rig, I thought to myself, "Whoever named that did a good job. Because that thing is downright wacky and there's no way I'll ever fish it." It must have been invented by a kid who didn't know how to rig a worm properly. So junior just stuck the hook right through the centre. Little did they know a simple wacky-rigged soft plastic worm would be one of the most deadly fishing techniques on the water. I said I wouldn't be caught dead with one, but I've been wrong before, and I have to admit this is a rig I won't be caught dead without. And the crazy thing about it is anyone can fish it. All you do is cast it out and let it slowly sink to the bottom.

There are two different ways to rig a wacky worm. One of them is to run the hook through the centre of the bait at a 90-degree angle and the other way is to run the hook through the centre of the bait, with the hook point parallel to the worm, leaving the hook point in the worm. Each way of rigging offers a different action and the parallel method also allows for a more weedless presentation. Wacky, but true.

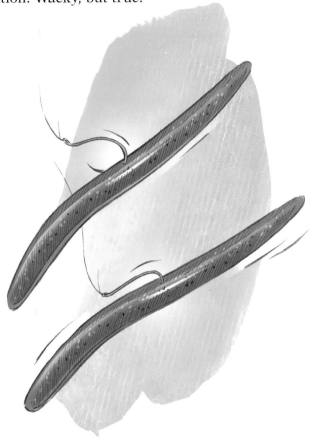

TIP 53:
Go Shallow with Crankbaits

When most anglers think of using a crank, they think of fishing in deeper water. But there's no reason to limit yourself. A crankbait can be one of the most effective shallow-water baits out there. One of the reasons they seem to be so effective in the shallows is that few people fish them there.

Most manufacturers these days have come out with shallow-running crankbaits in their lineups. But something you can do to any crankbait to make it run shallow is heat up the bill and bend it inwards towards the body of the bait. This will drastically reduce the depth at which your bait runs and will give you a totally custom bait that nobody else has.

TIP 54:
Guard Your Guides

It just makes sense — you want to protect your rod, especially your rod guides. You don't want to get cracks or scratches in them, because eventually that's going to damage your line, and damaged line means lost fish. A lot of anglers simply hook the bait to their guide when they're done fishing. Don't do it. Do yourself a favour and hook it on the guide frame so as not to damage the ceramic insert.

TIP 55:
You Reely Gotta Do It

A reel is basically like any other mechanical device. You wouldn't drive your truck for an entire year without servicing it — would you? If you do, maybe you should read your truck's manual, because you're going to need it.

Yearly reel maintenance is one way of ensuring your expensive investments will last for years. If you're comfortable taking mechanical things apart, tear your reels down all the way and soak the parts in a water-soluble degreaser like Simple Green. Then rinse them with water, dry them and put them back together. Use a high-quality reel oil for the bearings and a heavy gear grease for the main gear and pinion gear. If you're not comfortable doing this, send your reels to an authorized reel repair company and have them do it. There's nothing that will make your reels last longer and give you more satisfaction on the water than well-maintained equipment.

TIP 56:
Use Silicon Spray with Your Line

One thing I know about is conditioner — I use a lot of it. Hey, if you're going to have a TV fishing show like me, you have to look good and conditioner helps me do that. Obviously I'm not talking about hair conditioner — I gave up on that years ago. What I'm talking about is line conditioner. It can be your best friend.

Old line and even new line can be unwieldy — especially heavier lines. One way to keep line soft and supple is to use a silicon line conditioner like Kevin VanDam's Line & Lure Conditioner. This product has been chemically formulated to absorb into your line and make it softer and more manageable.

TIP 57:
Knot Tricks

Improperly tied knots can result in losing that fish of a lifetime. Here are a couple of tips to help you tie better knots and get your trophy into the boat. Because knots have a tendency to heat the line when cinching down, place a little spit (if you're a gentleman you can use a little scent) on the knot just before you cinch it down. The fluid acts as a lubricant and dissipates the heat of friction.

Also, when tying a Palomar Knot, begin to cinch the knot by pulling on both the tag end and main line until the knot is down by the eye of the hook. At this point, pull only the tag end to complete the cinching of the knot. This little trick ensures that only the part of the line that's going to be discarded is heated up and not the main line.

TIP 58:
To the Point

Success in fishing, as in any sport, often comes down to the small things. A hook point is about one of the smallest details but it can make the biggest difference. Hook points may look like they're sharp but anglers need to check with more than their eyes to be sure a hook is ready for the heat of battle. First, check to ensure the point hasn't rolled back. Take the hook in question and run it over your finger from barb to point. If the hook point has rolled back, you'll feel it grab the skin on your finger. If it hasn't, you're good, and it's time to determine whether it's sharp. You'll need to run the point along your thumbnail. If the hook wants to grab your nail, the hook is sharp. If not, it needs to be sharpened or replaced.

TIP 59:
Tungsten vs. Lead

You know that old saying, "You get what you pay for"? Well, it's absolutely true. There has been much debate as to whether or not tungsten weights are worth their price. Let me tell you — yes they are. What tungsten brings to the table is a more compact sinker that has less drag in the water and through vegetation. And, because tungsten is much harder than lead, it gives an angler more sensitivity while working the bait across the bottom.

TIP 60:
Rattle Your Bait

Fish have ears — they don't look like they do, but they do. And they use them to find food. So, if you're fishing dirty water, one way to make a bait easier for a fish to find is to use small insert rattles in your soft plastics or clip-on rattles on your jigs. Most tackle shops, like Bass Pro Shops, offer many sizes available in either glass or hard plastic. For soft plastics, simply push the rattle into the body of the worm or grub. And in the case of jigs, place the rattle collar under the skirt and attach the rattle. Either way, you now have a bait that fish will come looking for even when they can't see.

TIP 61:
Toothpick Trick

Later in this book you're going to read a tip where I tell you that toothpicks are useless for pegging sinkers and that you should use a bobber stopper instead. But don't throw those toothpicks away, because they do have a use.

If you're having problems with your worms sliding down the hook, here's a good tip for you. Carry some flat toothpicks and use them to peg the head of the worm to the eye of the hook. To do this, simply push the pointed end of a toothpick through the worm, through the eye of the hook and back out the other side of the worm. Then cut the toothpick flush with the sides of the worm. Now you have a bait that won't slide down the shaft of the hook.

TIP 62:
Buoyant Baits for Carolina Rigs

There are a few manufacturers that make soft baits that float. These baits work well behind a Carolina rig because they will float a hook and stay above the bottom, where fish are more apt to see them. But if you don't have a bait that floats, or you want to make one of your favourite baits float, you can do so by adding a small piece of foam to the shank of your hook before you run the hook point back into the bait. It's a great way to keep your bait off the bottom.

TIP 63:
Texpose Your Hook

Have you ever set the hook on a worm fish and upon examining your worm or craw noticed the hook point never penetrated the plastic? Well, this little problem can be alleviated by Texposing your hook instead of leaving the point buried in the plastic.

To Texpose a hook, simply run the hook point through the bait and straighten the worm out so it has no bends in it. At this point, pull on the worm where the hook point exits the plastic and run the point through the skin of the bait just in front of the hook point. As you let go of the plastic, the bait will relax and cover the point of the hook. Now your hook point has to penetrate only a thin skin of plastic instead of the entire bait.

Texpose Your Hook

TIP 64:
Be a Slacker

If you haven't heard of a tube, or don't know what it is, you either just started fishing or you've been living under a rock. Over the past twenty years, the lowly tube has become one of the mainstays of bass fishing, but it didn't originate with bass at all. In fact, it was originally developed as a crappie bait.

Bobby and Garry Garland started the tube craze when they saw how effectively their mini-jigs worked for crappie. They felt that since a bass is just an over-grown sunfish, the mini-jigs would work for bass too. So they put together a bigger, thicker mini-jig and called it a Fat Gitzit. The name morphed over time and the genre of lures became known as the tube bait.

Tubes can be used for flipping, skipping and, when rigged with a tube head, can be fished over deep reefs like the ones in Lake Erie. The tube's versatility is what makes it such a fish-catching machine. It's not just a bait for largemouth and smallmouth bass — this bait works wonders on walleye, trout and steelhead, and muskie and pike anglers are even throwing giant tubes now.

This bait definitely works for just about everything that swims. One of the simplest tips that will help you cash in on tube success is to just let the bait fall on a slack line. I know what you're thinking. The whole time you were growing up your granddaddy told you to keep the line tight so you'd know when a fish hit. But don't worry about keeping your line tight. A tube is soft and the fish will hold on to it for a long time. In any case, you'll definitely get more hits if you let this bait fall on a slack line. The slack line allows the bait to fall on a spiral and that action drives fish crazy.

TIP 65:
Curly or Straight?

Just like any other bait, choosing the perfect worm can be a daunting task. Not only do these things come in thousands of colours, they come in different shapes and sizes. The two most common shapes are a straight tail and a curly tail. I most often use straight-tail worms in colder months, when the fish are looking for something a little less active. The curly tail seems to be a better option in the warmer months or in dirty water, because the extra action of the tail makes it easier for the fish to find the bait. One thing people don't think about when choosing a worm is where they're fishing. If you find yourself in a really weedy area, always try to fish a straight-tail worm because it's easier to get your bait through the vegetation without getting its tail wrapped up in it.

TIP 66:
Feel Your Crank

Everybody has them in their tackle boxes — beautiful, shiny crankbaits. But many anglers don't fish them. Why they have them, I don't know. But a lot of anglers are intimidated by these baits, because they have six hooks just waiting to snag ten bucks' worth of fancy lure on the bottom of a lake. I would recommend worrying a little less. One thing to remember is that although a crankbait has all those hooks, it's not going to snag up nearly as much as you think it will if you fish it properly. A crankbait's bill actually works as a guard for most cover. You can bang it off wood, rocks and weeds and not worry about getting hung up — again, if you fish it properly. How you do this is by paying attention to how things feel on the end of your line. If you feel that your bait is hitting weeds, stop reeling and it will float up and away from the weeds. Once it clears the cover, start cranking again. If you learn how a crank is meant to feel, you'll be amazed at the types of things this bait can swim through.

TIP 67:
Does Size Matter?

Well, size definitely plays a big role in bait selection. I don't care whether you're fishing a crankbait, spinnerbait, a worm or a drop shot—in most situations you want to make your bait look like what the fish are used to seeing. Early in the year baitfish are at their smallest. So it only makes sense to use smaller baits. As the season progresses, the bait gets bigger, and that's when you need to increase the size of your lures.

TIP 68:
The One-Two Punch

When fishing any fast-moving retrieve bait like a jerkbait or topwater bait, it's good to have a second rod rigged and ready with a bait like a Senko or a tube in the event you have a fish follow the lure you're bringing back to the boat. Sometimes a fish will follow a fast-moving bait but won't eat it. Drop an unweighted Senko or a tube on the fish and it may find the second bait too hard to resist.

The key with this technique is to be ready. If you waste your time stumbling around looking for the drop bait, the fish is going to lose interest. Some team tournament anglers have this one-two punch approach down to a science. If your buddy's ready, your missed opportunity can turn into a caught fish for him.

TIP 69:
Shhh . . . Be Very, Very Quiet — We're Hunting Fish

Anglers who fish out of boats seem to be really careful about being quiet. But for some crazy reason I see shore anglers banging their feet down the bank, making all sorts of noise and thinking it has no effect on the fish. Don't get me wrong, I'm not the quietest dude you've ever met. However, the time in my life when I am quiet is when I'm fishing from the shore. When approaching your fishing spot, don't bang your feet along the bank — walk lightly. By banging your feet you're sending vibrations through the ground and into the water, warning any fish that is nearby of your presence.

TIP 70:
Spinnerbait Stripdown

Spinnerbaits are one of the best lures to use for covering a lot of water and finding fish. The problem is that most anglers take the spinnerbait out of the package, tie it on their rod and use it without ever adjusting the bait to meet their needs. One of the best tips for using a spinnerbait that works when the fish get locked in on smaller baitfish is to remove some strands of the skirt from the bait to decrease its volume. You can also cut the skirt down shorter to more closely resemble the size of the bait you're trying to imitate.

TIP 71:
Don't Be a Fool, Adjust Your Spool

It happens every year — anglers take their annual pilgrimage to their local tackle superstore and find themselves entranced by shiny new pieces of fishing mechanics. In their minds, the brand-new Acme B2000-28 Super Baitcaster is the only thing standing between them and the cover of *Field and Stream*. By the time spring rolls around and the final mortgage payment on the reel has been made, they're ready to take their rightful place atop the angling food chain. Unfortunately, what starts off as a dream quickly becomes a nightmare with a backlash big enough to make a bald eagle jealous.

Even with the latest and gratest gear, many anglers don't take the time to set up their bait-casting reels properly. One easy way to avoid disappointment is to adjust the spool-tension knob located on the handle side of the reel. To do this properly, string the rod up and tie a half-ounce jig to the end of the line. Hold the rod up, press the free-spool button and let the bait fall to the ground without your thumb on the spool. If the jig hits the ground and a small backlash happens, the spool knob isn't tight enough. If the lure doesn't fall, it's too tight. Adjust the knob so that the jig falls but the spool stops spinning when the jig hits the floor. Now you're ready to take the reel and fish it.

TIP 72:
Make It Stick

Some sports have performance-enhancing drugs. Not fishing — we're a clean and wholesome sport. However, we do have performance-enhancing lines. Braided line is one of the biggest improvements fishing has ever had. Everybody knows someone who just can't feel a fish bite. Braided lines have changed all of that. They have virtually no stretch, granting just about anyone the ability to feel a fish fart.

But many people have problems when they attach braid to their reels, because braid is slick and will spin on almost any reel spool. This can create a major problem when fighting a fish or even when retrieving a lure. In order to keep this from happening, put a few wraps of nylon monofilament on the spool first and then splice the braid to the monofilament. The nylon will grab the spool and not allow the braid to slip on it, and you'll catch more fish.

TIP 73:
Check It Out

I don't care if you're fishing a tournament, filming a TV show or trying to beat your brother at the annual family fish-off. Losing fish sucks.

One way to prevent this from happening is to check your line. I'm always checking mine — as often as every five or six casts if I'm fishing in an area with a lot of cover. This won't guarantee you'll never lose a fish, but it will save you from that "I should have checked my line" feeling when you break a good fish off at the side of the boat.

Your line is one of the most important connections between you and that trophy fish. So it makes sense to check it often for nicks and kinks. This is easily done by running the line between your forefinger and thumb, and feeling for rough spots on the line from the knot up about three feet. But cover and hang-ups aren't the only things that can kink line — a good backlash can too. In order to feel line that is only off the reel on a long cast, make a long cast and reel the line through your forefinger and thumb to feel for kinks and nicks that could have resulted from a backlash.

TIP 74:
See the World Through
Rose-Coloured Hooks

There's been a lot of talk over the recent years about coloured hooks — mainly red. Here's my deal. I've tried to test this and on one lake in particular (Erie), coloured hooks seem to really make a difference. I put the red hook on the back of a crankbait and most of the fish come on the back hook. Then I move the red hook to the front of the bait and most of the fish come on the front hook. That being said, I've talked to biologists and they tell me that red is the first colour that disappears underwater. So I can't tell you whether red hooks are going to make more fish strike or if I'm catching more on the red hook because the fish can't see it. But in some situations, red hooks seem to make a difference.

TIP 75:
Supersize Your Spinnerbaits

One of the coolest tricks in fishing is to show the fish something they're not used to seeing. While tons of anglers spend countless hours in their workshops trying to reinvent the wheel, sometimes it's something as simple as putting a bait in an area they're not used to seeing it.

Fish love spinnerbaits. But they're predominantly a shallow-water bait — unless you tweak them. A neat trick to add weight to a spinnerbait is to remove the core from a rubbercore sinker and place the sinker on the hook shaft of the spinnerbait. The weight is hidden behind the skirt, so you can add as much as a half an ounce to your favourite spinnerbait without affecting its profile or hooking ability. What you'll end up with is something the fish haven't seen before at those deeper depths, and it may turn out to be just what they were looking for.

Tree River

I have to be honest with you — being a professional fisherman and hosting a television show has got to be the greatest job in the world. One thing that blows me away is all the off-the-wall stuff that happens while we're shooting. We've had camera guys fall in the icy spring waters of Lake Erie while shooting; we've even had paparazzi from local papers chase us down through the bushes to take pictures of me while I was fishing. But nothing was crazier than what happened to me while filming on the Tree River in Nunavut, Canada.

We had set out that day to fish a spot on the river called the Presidential Hole, a little more than three miles up the river — probably the hardest three miles I've ever hiked in my life. Not because of the distance or the giant arctic hills and valleys we had to trudge through. The reason I could hardly bring myself to keep going was that I didn't want to fish later, or further on. I wanted to fish right now.

The whole hike you're within sight of the Tree River, which is basically the most incredible arctic char river in the world. To top that off, the only thing more amazing than the fishery is the scenery — it's truly one of the few places I've been in my life where I literally could not believe I was there. These two things coupled with the fact that we were walking past other anglers fighting fish were driving me crazy! I just wanted to stop and fish. But we had a goal and that goal was to fish the Presidential Hole — aptly named due to the fact that former President George Bush fishes there. I figured if it was good enough for George, that's where I wanted to fish.

So we get up there — camera crew, make-up artists, lighting specialists — and everything is going to plan. The scenery is breathtaking and the fish are on fire. After catching two or three quick fish I couldn't believe how amazing this place was — it was definitely worth the hike. Then, out of nowhere, this fly-fishing dude shows up. We'd actually passed him earlier on our hike up the river while he was fighting a fish.

As he came up to us, he more or less demanded that we leave the spot because he wanted to fish it. Well, believe me, at no time do I think I own the world, or the river, and I have no problems sharing a spot with another angler. But this guy didn't want any part of sharing the spot — he wanted it all to himself. And the last thing I'm going to do is leave in the middle of a shoot.

Since I wasn't leaving, he decided that instead of sharing the water with me, it would be best if he stood behind the cameraman and stared at me while I fished. Now I don't get rattled by much, but it's definitely weird to have a guy give you the evil eye the whole time you're shooting a show. The funny thing is the more fish we caught, the madder he got. But the weirdest part of the story happened when he needed to go pee.

He was so bound and determined to get in the spot as soon as we left that when he needed to relieve himself, he didn't even bother turning his back to us. He just peed, looking straight at me, the whole time. At that point we were pretty much done. So I figured, "Piss on it." And we left.

TIP 76:
Get Out of My Face

Suspending baits drive fish crazy. Think about it. You're Billy the bass, Willy the walleye or Percy the pike, and along comes a baitfish, or what you think is a baitfish. You're swimming behind it and it's supposed to run or swim away, but it doesn't — it just stops in front of you. It's like putting a sub in front of me. Sure, you could leave it in front of my nose for ten or even twelve seconds, but after that it doesn't matter whether I'm hungry or not. I'm taking a bite.

Have you ever found that your suspending baits slowly float to the surface under certain conditions? This is because most suspending baits are made to suspend at a certain water temperature. But, you can get that bait back to neutral buoyancy by either adding small lead SuspenDots to the underside of your bait or by taking a short piece of lead wire and wrapping it around the shaft of the front or middle treble hooks.

TIP 77:
The Shades of Line

In some fishing situations, it seems the fish don't notice the line at all. They're on fire and you could throw a bait in the water and a fish is going to hammer it before the lure enters the water. Unfortunately, those times don't seem to come around very often. So it only makes sense to use a line that is less obvious to fish.

Line colour is a factor that many anglers don't pay attention to. I believe line colour can play a major role in whether you catch a limit or nothing. It's been my experience that green-coloured lines are best for ultra-clear water situations. In dirty waters, clear lines are fine and offer more visibility to the angler.

Something I've started to do this year is use the new red lines in deep water. People much smarter than me will tell you red disappears in water deeper than 14ft. All I know is it seems to work.

TIP 78:
Hook Care

I don't know if you know this or not, but fish hooks are made of metal and metal and water don't mix too well. Of course you know this — I was just reassuring myself of this fact. Anyway, because we all fish on or near the water (we kind of have to, right?), our stored hooks always have the chance of coming in contact with water, even the ones that weren't used that trip.

In order to keep your hooks free from rust, place your hook box in an area that will keep its contents dry. If, by chance, your hook box does get water in it, take out all the hooks and dry them as soon as you get home. There's nothing worse than having a couple hundred dollars' worth of hooks rust and become useless.

Another preventative measure is to add rust-inhibitor strips to your hook boxes. These actually remove moisture from the air. Don't kid yourself, it's not like you can add one of these strips to your box and not worry about getting your baits wet. But they do keep light moisture from rusting your hooks.

TIP 79:
Drop Shot 101

I remember the first time I saw the drop shot. It looked to me like a strange, highly technical method that was way over my head. My style of fishing most times is fairly simple — I use a lot of tried and true techniques. I'm not a crazy rig guy. Some guys I fish tourneys against are like mad scientists trying different rigs and baits, and some of them are the craziest rigs you've ever imagined. Well, like I said, I like to keep things simple and use things that work. But although I avoided it at first, I quickly learned that the drop shot is something that works and it's here to stay. And it really is a lot simpler than I initially thought.

Most anglers don't realize there's a proper way to tie the knot when drop-shotting, and because of this many anglers don't have the luck with the rig that they should. First off, the best knot for the drop-shot rig is the Palomar Knot (see Tip 9). To tie it properly, follow these simple instructions.

First off, make sure you run the doubled line through the "hook-point" side of the eye. Then tie

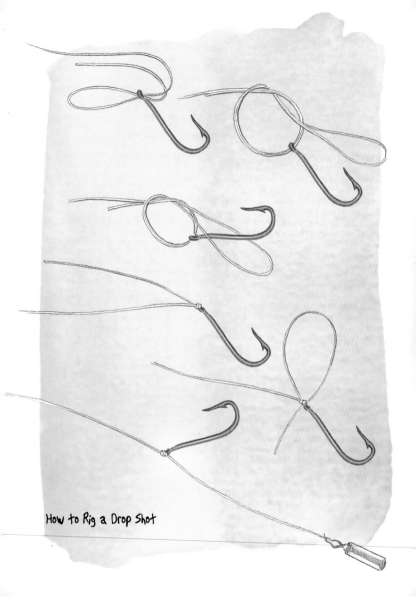

How to Rig a Drop Shot

the Palomar Knot as you would any other time. Once you have the knot cinched down take the tag end (that's the extra line that you'd normally cut off), and run it back through the hook-point side of the eye. By doing this, the hook will lie on the line with the point facing upwards. If you don't do this, your hook will lie to the side or downward and will be a lot less likely to hook fish. Finally, attach the weight to the tag end. Rigged this way, you'll notice a drastic increase in your hookups.

TIP 80:
Sticky Situation

Weightless baits are something most fish can't pass up. But sometimes conditions just don't allow you to fish a bait weightless. Maybe there's too much wind, tide or whatever. Sometimes you need to add just a little weight to your weightless worm.

Well, a number of companies make a waterproof clay that has tungsten powder incorporated into it. The clay is easily moulded by hand and will stick to your line and hooks. It's a great product to use when you want that jerkbait to sit nose-down or horizontal, and is also great when you need a little more weight on a fluke or a Senko.

TIP 81:
Split-Shot Rig

With the advent of the drop-shot rig, many people have forgotten one of the first true finesse rigs — the split-shot. Some anglers don't want me to tell you this, because the less a technique gets used on a body of water, the more effective it is.

The split-shot rig differs from the drop-shot rig in that the sinker, a split shot, is placed above the hook. With the sinker above the hook, the bait, normally a small plastic worm, leech or fluke, can float and glide naturally behind the sinker.

What makes this rig so good is the small weights and baits used. When fish have been heavily pressured from anglers or bad weather and are inactive, the split-shot rig shines. To a worn-out fish, the small baits represent something easy to catch and the small weights are less obtrusive than a Carolina rig. Plus, because the weights are so small, a fish doesn't feel the drag of the sinker as much when it picks up the bait. One more thing — the lack of weight will make you work the bait slower so you can maintain bottom contact, which is another plus when using finesse techniques.

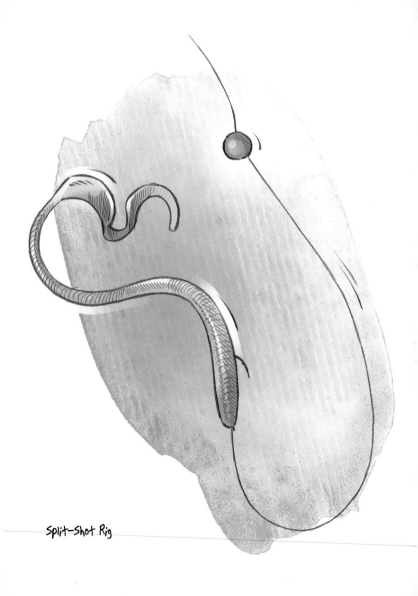

Split-Shot Rig

TIP 82:
To Bend or Not to Bend

You know that old saying, "They don't build them like they used to"? Well, when it comes to hooks a lot of that is true. We all started fishing round bends, but when manufacturers started making Z-bend hooks, a lot of anglers felt these were the best to use for Texas rigging.

I have always preferred round-bend hooks over Z-bends in most situations. The reason for this is that round-bend hooks have a much wider gap, and this allows for a more efficient hookset. The problem with Z-bend hooks is that although they seem to have a wider gap, they actually don't. On the typical Z-bend, the hook point is oriented straight towards the hook eye. Because of this, you don't utilize the gap as well as with a round-bend hook.

TIP 83:
Tube-Head Trick

Tubes can be rigged a number of different ways depending upon how you want to use them. One of the deadliest ways to rig them, though, is with a lead-head. Rigged with a leadhead where the hook eye is at a 90-degree angle from the shank, a tube will fall with an enticing spiral. It's this spiralling action that a tube is known for and it's something fish can't resist. Here's a cool tip on how to make your tube fall in wider spirals as it heads towards the bottom.

Insert a 90-degree head into your tube. Instead of pushing the head all the way to the nose of the tube, stop it halfway in and push the eye of the hook through the plastic. Because the eye is far away from the nose of the tube, it adds more resistance as the bait falls, thus making it fall in wider spirals.

TIP 84:
Less Is More

Fishing a grub on a jig is probably the most tried and true walleye method ever devised. Not only does this work for walleyes — just about every fish that swims will eat this setup. However, I see a lot of anglers who are overworking their grubs. When you're fishing a bait, think about what it's supposed to look like. A grub is basically supposed to be a minnow swimming across the bottom. When I see anglers jigging a grub, sometimes they are lifting it up to two feet off the bottom at a time. I don't know where you're fishing or what you're fishing for, but unless you're spending most of your time near a nuclear power plant outflow, make your bait look natural. Jig your bait an inch to two off the bottom at most. In most situations this is definitely going to help you catch more fish.

TIP 85:
Dredge the Bottom

When choosing a crank, one of the mistakes anglers make is the depth it fishes. In ten feet of water, most anglers will use a crank that runs eight to nine feet down, assuming they want a bait that runs right above the bottom. Most times, though, I'll throw a bait that runs deeper than the area I'm fishing. So, in ten feet of water, I want a bait that dives to twelve feet. By banging your bait off the bottom, you're going to trigger more strikes.

TIP 86:
If You Slack It, They'll Whack It

Jerkbaits, sometimes called twitchbaits, are one of the simplest baits to fish — in theory. I mean, what can be so hard about fishing these baits? You just fire them out and retrieve them with a jerk-jerk-pause, jerk-jerk-pause action, right? Well, that's how most people get taught to use them. I know I was. It wasn't until years later that I realized I was missing the boat with this technique.

One simple adjustment you want to make while fishing a jerkbait is to jerk the bait on a slack line. By leaving a bit of slack, you'll give the bait the freedom to sweep widely from side to side. Don't get me wrong, you'll catch fish some days by just throwing it out and jerking it back on a tight line, but if you leave the slack in your line you'll definitely find yourself catching more fish than your buddies.

TIP 87:
Bulging Blades

Colorado-bladed spinnerbaits are one of the most underutilized baits in fishing. These blades have a lot more vibration than other kinds, which makes them perfect for fishing in dirtier water or for slow rolling. The subtle, wide thump of these blades can drive fish crazy. They also allow you to keep the bait higher in the water column on a slow retrieve since they have more lift and are easier to bulge on the surface without the blades breaking the water.

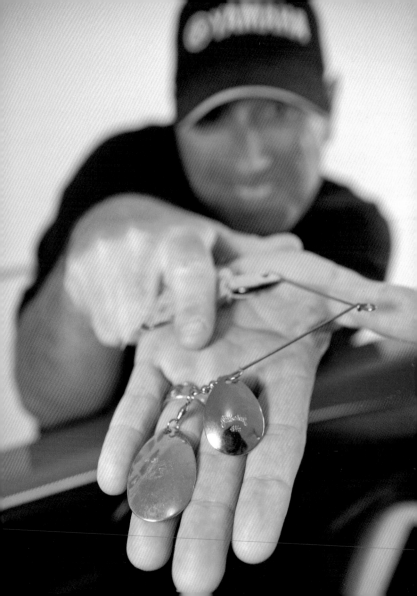

TIP 88:
Buddy Fish

Think about the last time you were out fishing with a buddy. He or she hooked into a fish — what did you do? If you're like the vast majority of anglers, chances are you just sat back and watched the show. But this isn't the time to watch the real-life fishing show going on in your boat. You have plenty of time to watch those when you're not on the water.

Oftentimes, when one fish is hooked, one or several other fish will end up following their doomed buddy. If your bait is there, these are remarkably easy fish to catch. Think about the last time you watched the fish in an aquarium feed. As soon as one eats it seems like they all get hungry, and they'll fight each other to get that food. This is what happens in real life much of the time. So when your buddy hooks that fish, make a cast towards his fish and try to capitalize on one of those followers.

TIP 89:
Change It Up

One thing a lot of anglers make a mistake with is their retrieve. So many anglers just cast out their bait and wind it back to the boat, never thinking about changing the direction their bait is moving in. One of the best ways to trigger a bite on wary fish is to cast far past a target and steadily reel in the bait towards the target with the rod off to one side of the boat. As the bait gets to the target, switch the rod to the other side of the boat, changing the direction of the bait. Fish see this as the bait trying to move away, and this change in direction will often elicit a strike. This technique works with any bait like swimbaits, cranks and spinnerbaits.

TIP 90:
Clip Your Net

The most heartbreaking fish are lost right at the side of the boat. A lot of this happens when an angler goes to net a fish. You get excited and stab at the fish, or the netting actually dangles in the water and gets caught in the hooks. This becomes an even bigger problem when you're fishing for bigger fish with deeper nets.

One of the coolest little tricks you can do to help your net control is tie a downrigger release clip to the shaft of your net. This will allow you to clip the net to the release. When you're not using it it'll keep things tidier. And when it comes time to scoop your trophy catch, the release will keep the net out of the way, only releasing it once the weight of the fish is in the net.

TIP 91:
Anti-Tangle Trick

I don't know how it happens, but if you ever try to move an armload of rigged fishing rods, either from the truck to the boat or the boat to the garage, somehow they end up getting entwined, tangled and connected in ways that would seem impossible if you weren't looking at the mess with your own eyes. All this can be avoided simply by taking the free line that runs from the tip of the rod to your hookkeeper at roughly the midsection of the rod and wrapping the line around the rod. The guides keep the line from unwinding and also keep that free line from being able to tangle in the other rods.

TIP 92:
Trailer Hitch Tricks

I'll bet you I've spent hours of my life jumping up and down on the back bumper of my truck trying to release my trailer from the hitch. What a waste of time and energy that was. If you unhook your trailer and can't get the hitch to release, simply shift your car into reverse and back up. The trailer will disconnect without even moving.

TIP 93:
Line Up!

One of the coolest things about the sport of fishing is you never stop learning. And some of the hottest techniques out there were actually borrowed from other genres of fishing. This one comes from your friendly neighbourhood fly fisherman.

For those times when you want your line to float high on the surface — like when fishing topwater baits — take some silicon fly floatant and rub it into the first six feet of line from your lure. The silicon acts to repel the water and makes your line float like you've never seen before.

TIP 94:
Stop Weighting

Man, oh, man, whoever was in charge of naming fishing equipment sure missed the boat on some stuff. Every year millions of little pieces of rubber, sold as bobber stops, are actually being used to peg weights.

Pegging a sinker can be a pain, especially with tungsten weights. What I've found to be the best peg for a worm weight is a bobber stop. If you want to try it, first place a small rubber bobber stop on the line, follow it with your worm weight and hook, and then rig your worm or other soft plastic on the hook. Then, to peg the bait, simply slide the bobber stop down flush with the sinker and voila, it's pegged. This way, not only is your weight pegged, but if you find you'd like to give the weight some ability to move, all you have to do is move the bobber stop up the line. It's a very versatile way to peg your sinker. Plus it's safer on your line than wedging a toothpick in the sinker hole.

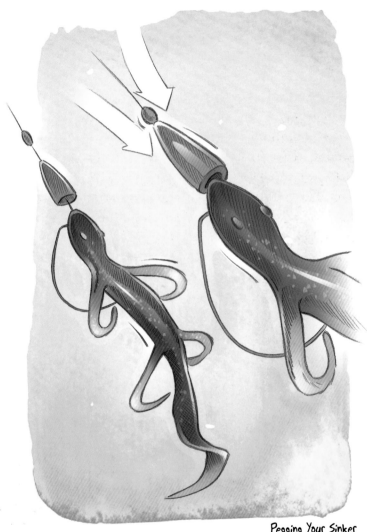

Pegging Your Sinker

TIP 95:
Stick It

Superglue is something I always have stowed in the boat. Two reasons: The first is that I left the cap off years ago and it's been stuck there ever since. The second reason is it's actually a great fishing tool. It allows me to repair soft plastic baits, it works to keep plastics from sliding down the shaft of the hook and it serves as a good method to stitch my skin up after an accident.

TIP 96:
Sinker Secret

The big problem with the drop-shot rig is keeping it stowed so it doesn't tangle with your other rods. Here's a quick and inexpensive way to keep your sinker attached to the rod so it doesn't make a mess when you're not using it. Go to the store, or have your wife or significant other do it if you're too embarrassed, and get yourself a couple of the elastic bands women use to tie their hair into ponytails. Slide the band on the end of your rod and place it by the bottom of your reel seat. Now you can slide your sinker under the band and it will hold the sinker firmly until you need that rod again.

TIP 97:
Electronic Eyes

Electronics are one of the most underutilized pieces of equipment in most anglers' boats. A lot of anglers have these units but don't spend much time learning how to use them.

Electronics are always a big plus when fishing, because they show the angler water depth, structure, bait, and even the fish. They are also an absolute must when fishing vertically below the boat in deep water. Situations where electronics become your eyes under the water include drop-shotting and spoon-fishing. Use your electronics to find these deep fish (or bait) and drop your lure straight down on top of the fish. If your electronics are set up properly, you can actually watch the lure and see how the fish react to it, and accurately keep your bait where the fish are.

TIP 98:
Spacing Your Shot

One of the crazy things about fishing is watching anglers spend countless hours trying different colours, shapes and sizes of baits when sometimes all they need is a little adjustment to the rig they're using. When it comes to a technique like split-shotting, placement of the shot from the hook is probably the most important part of the rig. Under really tough conditions, I find it best to place the shot anywhere from four to six feet from the hook. This allows the bait to act more naturally and also allows the fish more time to eat the bait without fear of it feeling the sinker.

Under not-so-tough conditions, or circumstances where the fish want the bait moved faster, rig the split shot anywhere from two to four feet from the hook.

TIP 99:
Keep Your Rig Steady

The best retrieve I've found when working a Carolina rig is a steady retrieve. Remember, with a technique like this, where the bait is actually floating, it's really easy to overwork your lure.

Because the size of the weight used with this rig, you can work it fast or slow, depending on the fishes' mood. The best technique for retrieving the setup is to move the rod to your side in one full sweeping motion. When you get to the end of the sweep, reel up the slack and begin another steady sweep. I prefer this over just reeling the bait in, because when you get a bite in the middle of a sweep, you can easily drop slack back into the line before you set the hook. When using a reeling retrieve, it's hard to accomplish this and you run the risk of the fish feeling pressure on the end of the line.

TIP 100:
Don't Hang Your Crank

The arch-nemesis of all anglers has to be the snag. Realistically, with today's lines, most snags can be pulled out — especially in weeds. However, if you want to have an easier time fishing a crankbait through weeds, simply remove one of the bends off the belly treble hook. To do this, hold the bait upside down (belly of the bait up) and lay the hook on the belly of the bait so the split ring allows the

hook to rest straight, one hook pointing up. Take a pair of sidecutters and cut this hook off at the shaft. This will still leave two points to hook the fish but they will run along the sides of the bait in more of a weedless fashion.

Dave's FISHING TALES

Minnow Bucket

People like to debate what the toughest sport is. Is it football? Maybe hockey? Or is it rugby? To me, I find it strange that fishing is never included in that list. Those other sports have one thing that fishing doesn't have — restrooms. I mean, if a hockey player needs to go to the can, he simply slides off to the changeroom without anyone noticing — no big deal. Lack of that luxury not only makes our sport the toughest, but puts an angler in some unique situations.

One time in particular, I was out on my home lake, Lake Scugog, pre-fishing for an upcoming bass tournament. Scugog is basically a giant, shallow, muddy swamp — but it's also the home to some giant largemouth bass. Because of this, it gets a ton of fishing pressure and good anglers quickly learn that the harder you're willing to work, the better the reward. And one of the best tricks is to manoeuvre way back into the shallow, swampy areas where most anglers wouldn't dare to venture.

One day, while back in one of these secluded honey-holes, I suddenly found myself in a real predicament. Everything up until that time had been perfect — the weather was nice, the fish were biting. And then out of nowhere — ERUGGHH — I had an abrupt feeling in my lower abdomen that proved to me that bowels don't have eyes. If they did, they would have known that we were nowhere near a restroom or anything that resembled one. Unfortunately they didn't have ears either to listen to my pleas for a few minutes to get back to civilization — to them it was poop time.

It was at that point that I remembered a story I once read in *Reader's Digest* — ironically I had read this particular story while pooping. This bit of cutting-edge journalism mentioned that one could make a feeling like mine pass by sitting on a hard surface. So that's what I did, and it actually worked. So I got right back up and continued fishing.

Life was good again — for about ten minutes. This time, though, that insistent feeling was back with a vengeance and there was no relieving it, hard surface or not. A few minutes earlier I had been in control of the situation. Now my bowels were calling the shots. The problem was, going to shore wasn't an option. I'd never make it. And I'm a little too top-heavy to crouch over the side of the boat unless I want to fall into a puddle of my own poop.

As the sweat ran from my brow and the pain in my stomach grew stronger and stronger, I realized that I was going to poo and I was going to poo right now, whether I liked it or not.

As I looked around my boat in panic for something, anything, that could help me, I saw it out of the corner of my eye. It seemed to glow like the Holy Grail. I swear, for a fleeting moment, I heard angels singing as I approached it — the minnow bucket.

Now, your average yellow minnow bucket probably sells for about eight bucks. But at that moment you probably could have charged me thousands to use it. I positioned the yellow receptacle, dropped my drawers and the rest is history. Unfortunately, one of the things I didn't think through before soiling up my bright yellow minnow bucket was what I was going to do with it afterwards. Let me say this — I don't litter and I don't condone littering. But in this particular situation, I really had no choice. I grabbed my trusty bucket and dropped it off the side of the boat. As it floated away, I walked back up to the front deck of my boat and went back to fishing.

About an hour later, all thoughts of my minnow bucket free from my mind, things were going well. I'd caught a few more fish. Then I heard in the distance the buzz of an outboard motor. I thought nothing of it, but as that buzz got closer and closer, I began to hear some yelling over the engine — that's when I turned to check what was going on.

There were two guys on the boat and they were headed down to the area I'd just finished fishing. Then I saw it. These two guys were heading straight towards a bright yellow object floating in the water. And not only were they heading towards it, the guy in the front of the boat was pointing at it. I couldn't hear what they were saying, but he may as well have been yelling, "Poopberg, straight ahead!" — they were on a collision course. I thought, "What should I do?" With that, I did what most other people would do in this situation — I got my binoculars out to watch the show.

As I focused in on them, I saw that the guy in the front of the boat was stretched out with both hands, trying as hard as he could to grab that bobbing, yellow minnow bucket. He obviously thought he had found himself a treasure or maybe some free bait. Little did he know my yellow minnow bucket contained a mudshark. He finally grasped the handle, raised it into the air and that is the point at which I heard the loudest &$@*!! I have ever heard in my life! He scared birds out of trees and frogs off lily pads. That day I learned two things — don't ever go fishing without a minnow bucket, and never, ever grab somebody else's.

TIP 101:
Never Leave a Good Bite

Okay, think about the last time you had one of those mornings. You know those mornings we all dream about, when the lake is just alive and you're catching fish after fish. Inevitably, after a while, the fish just stop biting. Oftentimes, anglers pack away their rods and assume the action is over.

Never ever leave an area where you've been catching fish, even if they have stopped biting, without first trying a different bait or colour. Sometimes that little different approach is all that's needed to trigger the fish to start eating again.

TIP 102:
Rip It Good

One area where rattle (vibration) baits really shine is ripping them through the weeds. Unfortunately, a lot of anglers hear about this and go out and try it with their traditional crankbaits, and the result is a disaster. This is where vibration baits like a Rattlin' Rapala shine.

When ripping a rattlebait, you want to use a stiffer rod and braided line. This gives you the power to be able to pop your bait and a fish out of the weeds once you hook it. This technique really gives a lot of anglers a hard time. Many anglers don't rip the bait near hard enough because they can't get their head around the fact that a fish will hit a bait that's flying over its head at 90 miles per hour. However, it's that quick, ripping retrieve that triggers the strike. So don't be timid when ripping a vibration bait through the grass.

TIP 103:
Change Is a Good Thing

I know some reels come with line, but that's not the line that should live there for the rest of the reel's life. A ton of recreational anglers pick up their new rod and reel combo, get the clerk to spool on some new line, and figure they're good until it's gone.

Lines have changed for the better over the last few years but that doesn't mean they're infallible. I still change my nylon line after a hard day of use no matter what. Fluorocarbon lines, on the other hand, are more resilient and can be fished anywhere from five to ten times before changing. Braid is probably the best line for those who don't like changing their lines — it can be changed annually.

TIP 104:
The Weight Inside the Bait

We all spend a bunch of time trying to avoid snags. Let's face it, fish live near cover and if you want to catch fish, you have to fish in the cover. Tubes are a great bait and Texas-rigging them will allow you to effectively fish them in a lot more areas. Unfortunately, in a lot of situations, worm weights make the bait look bigger than you'd like.

This is the perfect application for an insert tube weight. These are weights that can be inserted into the body of the tube and are held in place by an EWG (extra wide gap)-style hook. By rigging a tube this way, you get the weedless properties of any Texas-rigged bait but without the external sinker, making the bait more realistic and manageable.

TIP 105:
Quick Connect

A number of sinkers can work for drop-shotting — bell sinkers, rubbercore sinkers and split shot can all be used. But the best sinker, by far, is the quick-connect drop-shot sinker. Nearly every sinker company makes these now and they are available in both lead and tungsten. You know a technique works when all the companies design a sinker for it.

The beauty of these sinkers is you don't need to use a knot to connect them, and if you get hung up, you can pull your line through the clip and get your hook and bait back. The other cool thing is the clip allows you to move your sinker up and down your tag end without having to retie your rig.

I've also had times when a fish ate my bait, got hooked and pulled the line through the clip all while I was snagged on the bottom and trying to get the rig loose. If I hadn't been using a sinker that had the quick-connect clip, those fish would more than likely have broken off.

TIP 106:
Everything's Bigger in Texas

The Texas rig is probably the best-known rig used for worm fishing. This is most likely because of its versatility — it can be used for flipping or working deep structure. The Texas rig is an easy rig to learn and one every bass angler needs to know how to use.

How to Rig a Texas Rig

1. Insert the hook through the nose of the bait.
2. Rotate the hook out the bottom of the bait.
3. Push the hook through the bait at a point where it will lie straight.
4. Slide the bait onto the bend of the hook. The bait should lie straight with no twist between the eye and the hook bend.

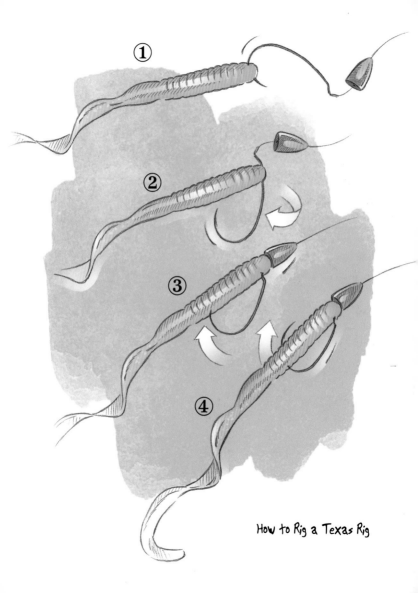

① ② ③ ④

How to Rig a Texas Rig

TIP 107:
Split-Shot Hooks

Because the split-shot rig is used with small baits and light line, it's very important to use light-wire hooks, like an Eagle Claw Aberdeen-style hook. Because the baits are small, the light-wire hook allows the bait to act more naturally in the water. And because you're using light line you don't have to worry about the hook straightening as it sets or when a big fish turns.

TIP 108:
Straight into a Fish's Mouth

When anglers first rig their worm, they will take extra care and precautions to make sure that worm is straight. Inevitably, the worm slides down the shank and becomes crooked as you fish it. A lot of anglers will turn a blind eye to that. If you want to catch more fish, always straighten out your worm if you notice it's slid down the shank. A crooked worm won't fall right and can also add twist to your line if you're using lighter lines.

TIP 109:
Up or Down?

Grubs have to be one of the most effective baits known to man. You can literally catch anything that swims on this bait. When it comes to rigging it, I will always place it tail-down with respect to the hook.

The reason is the bait will have a lot more action on the fall and as you're slowly reeling it in.

TIP 110:
Feed Your Cranks

One of the most deadly tricks you can do when fishing a crankbait is to feed the fish your lure. What do I mean? Well, I'll tell you. Most people throw a crankbait and just crank it on a steady retrieve. If you stop your bait and feed it slack, most crankbaits will actually spin completely around and end up facing the opposite direction. This drives fish crazy, and it's something that very few anglers do.

TIP 111:
Learn from the Last One

Every year I watch anglers hit the lake. The shore anglers line up, rear back on their rods and cast as far out to the middle of the lake as they can — all believing that if they could just cast another five feet farther they'd catch a whole lot more fish.

Then you have the anglers with their brand-new boats. They head out in the lake, rear back on their rods and cast as close to the shore as they possibly can — all of them believing that if they could just cast a little closer, they'd catch more fish. Well, I guess that's just human nature — the grass is always greener on the other side.

If you're fishing from the shore, pay attention to where you catch your fish. If I cast out 30 feet and find I'm catching all my fish 10 feet from shore, chances are those first 20 feet are dead water. There's a reason those fish are sitting 10 feet from shore. Maybe it's a drop-off, weeds or some other cover or structure. The smart tip to take from this is to start making your casts parallel to shore in the 10-foot area, keeping your bait where the fish are for a longer period of time.

TIP 112:
Willow Leaf Lowdown

Spinnerbaits are one of today's most popular baits. Not only are they easy to fish, but their safety-pin design allows them to be incredibly weedless. In order to make your spinnerbait even more weedless, try using willow leaf blades on it. Their tight rotation keeps the blades from tangling in the weeds, yet they still give off a lot of flash.

TIP 113:
Riggin' Rods

Carolina rigging is an awesome technique and as close to live-bait fishing as you'll get. One of the biggest problems anglers have with this technique is hooking fish once they bite. That's because most anglers make a long cast when they use this technique. For that reason, you want to be using a long, stout rod when fishing this rig. I like something in the medium-heavy to heavy range and at least seven feet in length. This will allow you to make a hookset even on a 70-foot cast.

TIP 114:
Speed and Direction

Some people love it, some people hate it — trolling. The one thing you can't deny is that it catches fish. The guys who hate it will tell you it's because there's less skill involved with trolling than with other styles of fishing. Me, I just want to catch fish. Whatever is working, I'll do. One simple thing you can do to turn the odds in your favour is vary your speed and direction. Many fish are caught by an angler after their motor stalls, or they abruptly change direction. These changes in speed and direction trigger a fish to strike. Think about it — if a bait is going to be trolled for miles, a fish can swim behind it for miles without eating. Every once in a while, if you add that trigger-effect you'll quickly cash in on some trolling trophies.

TIP 115:
Get a Grip on the Chips

Unfortunately, some of the best fishing spots in the world are found in some of the most rural locations. Spend any time trailering a boat down a gravel road and you'll quickly learn that those little stones will wreak havoc on your boat trailer. One easy way to avoid this problem is to have your trailer coated with the same rubber spray material they use on pickup bed liners. This will keep the rocks from chipping the paint.

TIP 116:
"X" Marks the Spot

Some pro anglers dread marker buoys. Why? They feel as soon as they throw in one of those yellow or orange beacons, they'll be summoning other anglers into their secret honey-hole. I even know some pros who have taken these yellow or orange buoys and replaced them with duck or seagull decoys. Regardless of what they think, marker buoys can definitely help you catch more fish.

Fishing is no different from any other sport. Once you find something that brings you success, duplicate it and chances are you'll get more. If I find a rock pile or weedline or some other piece of structure that's holding fish, I will try and mark it right away so I can sit back and continue casting to the area. Anglers don't give fish near enough credit. You need to be right on the spot. I've fished areas in the past that if your cast was three feet away it might as well have been a mile away. The fish weren't moving. Hit them on the head with your lure, though, and it was lights out.

TIP 117:
Breakin' Wind

Anglers often find themselves intimidated by the wind, and for obvious reasons. It definitely makes boat control and fishing in general a lot more difficult. However, when fishing large flats or shoals, the wind can be your friend. The wind actually allows you to cover these large areas quickly and effectively. Some days the wind is just too strong and your drift is too fast. That's when it becomes imperative to use a drift sock. These are basically underwater parachutes that fill with water and slow down and control your drift so you can fish the area effectively without having to use your trolling motor to manoeuvre your boat.

TIP 118:
Underarm Roll Cast

It happens thousands of times a year. Two buddies get in the boat, line up aside each other, whip back their rods and begin an overhand long-bomb casting competition. This can be fun, but chances are, if you're fishing the shallows, when that bait crashes into the water with a thundering splash the fish will head in the other direction. In shallow water, it's almost always better to use an underarm roll cast. This allows you to keep your bait just above the surface, and when you finally do stop it, it falls gently into the water. It will also allow you more accurate casts and, most likely, catch you a few more fish.

TIP 119:
Ring It

Crazy amounts of fish are caught on wacky-rigged soft plastics. I know some people who hardly fish anything but this bait. About the only drawback this technique has is that you're going to go through a few

more baits than normal. One way to combat that is by using a plastic O-ring around the centre of the bait where you place the hook. Not only will this save you baits, it's also a simple way to add a little weight to your bait as well.

TIP 120:
Boat Ramp Rendezvous

Anglers spend countless hours searching for the ultimate fishing hot spot. One of the craziest things is, once you've launched your boat, you probably just left one. Boat ramps are one of the best spots to pick up a couple of quick and easy fish. I've never caught a ton of fish at boat ramps, but there's usually a few living nearby. Why? Because boat ramps are notorious for having a deep depression at the end of the ramp due to the motors kicking up sand, mud or gravel. Another reason why these areas usually hold fish is that although it's illegal in some areas, many anglers dump their unused live bait at the end of the trip, creating a free meal for any fish in the area.

TIP 121:
Crankbait Wrap

Crankbaits have to be one of my favourite baits to throw for anything that swims. Some people will call them dummy baits. Why? Because any old dummy can go out, cast them and reel in a fish. Hmm, maybe that's why I like them so much. However, one of the drawbacks with a crankbait is transporting it with all those hooks. With most baits, you just hook it to the hookkeeper on your rod and don't worry about it. With a crank, you'll have a lot less trouble with tangles if you invest in a lure wrap and use it.

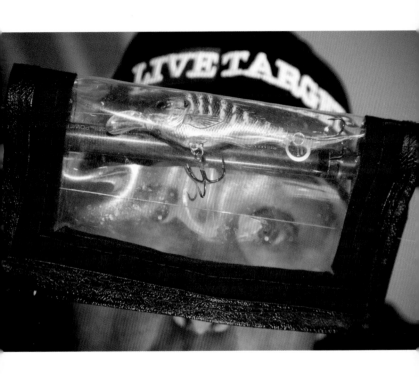

TIP 122:
Gettin' Grubby with It

If you're looking for a quick way to add a little colour or action to your spinnerbait, one of the easiest things you can do is add a grub as a trailer. Not only will this give your spinnerbait more bulk and colour, but it can also be that extra little action to trigger that finicky fish into eating.

A Grub as a Trailer

TIP 123:
Deadsticking

One of the techniques I have the hardest time with is deadsticking a worm. If you spend any time with me you realize I'm one of the most hyper freak-jobs you've ever met. So doing nothing with a bait is not very easy for me. But deadsticking a worm is sometimes one of the most deadly techniques on the water. Simply cast your bait out, let it sink to the bottom — and do nothing. When conditions are cold and fish are inactive, leaving a bait in front of them for an extended period of time could be just the ticket.

TIP 124:
The Carolina Rig

The Carolina rig is one of the most widely used rigs anywhere, yet not much credit is given to this great technique. That's because a lot of pro anglers consider it one step above live bait, since it doesn't take much talent to fish it. But I don't care about that. I like to catch fish and, because you're reading this tips book, I'm sure you do too.

The Carolina rig is a great technique to use when fishing vast flats or when you want to cover a lot of water fast with a soft plastic bait. The rig can be used in any depth of water. I normally use a one-ounce egg sinker when I'm using a Carolina rig, but there are times, like when I'm fishing really shallow water, when I'll step down to a smaller half-ounce weight.

Leader length is also a factor when Carolina rigging. Normally I use a four-foot leader, but under tough conditions I'll increase to six feet. It all depends on what the fish want, and to figure that out you have to experiment for yourself.

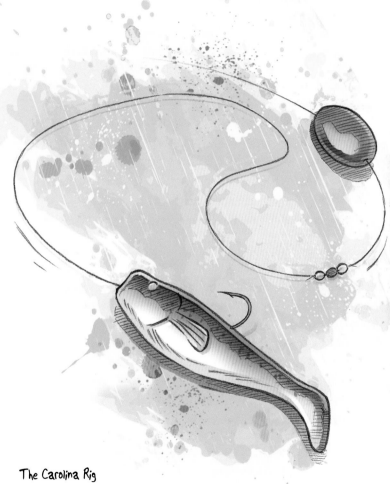

The Carolina Rig

TIP 125:
Keep It Right

Have you ever been driving down the road and witnessed somebody with a rod and reel in the back window of their car? You probably thought to yourself, "Hey, there's a hardcore angler. He has his rod and reel with him at all times. No matter what fishing opportunity should arise, he's ready to pounce." When I see that, though, my thoughts are a little different. I think, "Hey, there's a heartbroken angler. He's ready to get beat up on by a bass or any other fish he runs into." While he may think he's ready for any situation, his line sits in the sun and gets weaker and weaker.

Line is a very delicate part of your fishing arsenal — again, it is the only thing between you and that trophy fish on your lure. Because of that, proper care of your line is very important. One thing every angler needs to pay attention to is how to store line, whether it be on reels or still on the spool. Line is very sensitive to high temperatures and the ultraviolet rays given off by the sun. So, to ensure your line maintains its original strength, store it away from direct sunlight and extreme heat.

Swamp Monster Meets Ninja

One thing that makes the sport of competitive fishing very different from most other sports is that nobody really gets to see exactly what happens throughout the day. And some days, as a professional angler, I am immensely grateful for that. But since you actually took the time and spent your hard-earned money to purchase this book, I feel it's only fair to expose you to one of the most embarrassing on-the-water disasters I was ever involved in.

The disaster happened while fishing a pro-am tournament, which is basically an event where you welcome a stranger, the amateur, into your boat to fish with you. This particular event was a team pro-am, so we were actually working together — and you know what? We made a pretty good team.

By one o'clock on day one of the event, we found ourselves with a pretty decent weight of fish in the boat. I knew if I could just get two big bites we'd definitely find ourselves in the top five, and I knew just where we could get them.

In pre-fish I'd found a reed bed that didn't have many fish, but the ones it did have were huge. My plan going into the event was that if I got into a situation where I was one or two big bites away from a good finish, I could go to my secret little reed patch and seal the deal. It was time to head to my honey-hole.

As I rounded the corner and headed back into the bay that sheltered the spot I was counting on, my smile grew bigger and bigger — there were no other anglers in there. I was going to have the area all to myself! Everything was going exactly how I'd planned it.

As we slowly approached the reeds, I jumped up to the front deck of my boat and began firing a soft plastic jerkbait through the area that I knew was home to the fish I needed. And, just as I had envisioned, one of the resident giants bit my lure.

When the fish struck, I reared back and set the

hook and no matter how hard I pulled, I couldn't move it! All I felt was its enormous head thrashing back and forth — this fish was a giant — and with every thrash, I got even more excited.

Sometimes when you're fishing amongst reed beds, if you can't get a fish to come to you, you have to go to it. And that was the case with this fish as it tangled itself and my line in the reeds. In order to avert disaster, I slammed my trolling motor on high speed, stepped on the pedal and quickly began crashing through the reeds towards my monster fish. I made sure to keep pressure on the giant and as the boat got closer, I could see the fish on the surface. All I had to do was get to the fish and it was mission accomplished!

After what seemed like an hour, reeds and mud flying everywhere, I was finally right over the fish. But, as I leaned down to grab it, at that split second, my hook shook free and that's when my dream fish became a nightmare.

As I stood there in disbelief, I watched it, and some potential cash winnings, swim away deep into the reeds. As it turned out, though, that lost fish would be the least of my troubles.

After screaming profanities that shook the seagulls out of the trees for miles, I figured, "Okay, let's get back to fishing."

I stood up on the front deck of my boat, but this time I noticed something different — the boat wasn't moving at all. I'd been in such a hurry to chase down that fish that I'd actually jammed my boat on the bottom of the shallow reed bed. We were stuck — but hey, this happens sometimes. So, I did what every savvy angler who fishes a lot of shallow water does — I grabbed my push-pole. For those of you who don't know, a push-pole is a long pole that anglers use to move themselves quietly around the shallows or as an aid to get them dislodged from being grounded.

With push-pole in hand, I started pushing (and pushing) with all of my might — all to no avail. Then my amateur got involved. Still nothing. But, in my mind, everything was still under control.

Heck, I did have a 200-horsepower Yamaha on the back of my boat. I figured, "I'll just move us with the big motor." I jumped behind the wheel, started the motor and threw the boat in reverse. As it turned out, that wasn't the brightest idea I've ever had. All I did was coat the back deck of my boat in mud, reeds, and just about every other stinky piece of slime you could imagine that resides on the bottom of a swamp.

My next brilliant idea was to motor through the shallow reed patch — only this time in a forward fashion. Remember, I did have 200 horsepower! What was going to stop me?

Still sitting in the driver's seat, I threw the gear shift into forward, hit the accelerator and the boat came free — sort of. At this point, the boat was basically bunny-hopping through the reed bed, moving only inches at a time, but we were moving. Then, abruptly, the moving stopped. The boat sat motionless, high on a shallower spot than before.

Many of us professional anglers get stuck from time to time; it's just part of the game. But, there's being stuck and then there's being stuck. After my last bid for freedom, my boat wouldn't move an inch. I sat and pondered every possible option available with my partner and finally I realized I had no choice. I had to strip down to my underwear, in the middle of a tournament that only moments before I thought I was about to win, and jump in the water. My hope was that I could push from within the water while my partner used the push-pole from inside the boat and we could slowly free my shiny bass boat.

As soon as I hit the water I started wondering how in the world my boat could be stuck, because what I assumed would be hard, packed mud turned out to be a sludgy, stinky, filthy mess that swallowed my legs halfway past my knees. To top that off, I soon felt the slithering antics of the local residents — leeches, tadpoles and whatever the heck else lived in that water — crawling through my toes.

Trying to find the least mucky foothold I could, I walked around the boat and found the best position to push from. As I readied myself, I counted down with my partner and pushed with all my might. The boat didn't move an inch. Again we tried. Nothing. My beautiful, sparkling boat lay lifeless in the middle of this reed patch.

In desperation, I gave my partner a pep talk that would have made Vince Lombardi jealous. I knew if we only pushed hard enough, we could get the boat free, head back to weigh-in, and salvage our day with the fish we already had in the boat. So, on the count of three, my partner and I pushed again. I used every ounce of muscle I had and pushed harder than I've pushed anything in my life. I've heard stories of mothers who develop superhuman strength trying to lift cars off their trapped babies. Let me tell you — at this moment in my life, those mothers had nothing on me. Yet, the boat still wouldn't move. I continued to push, believing I couldn't be beaten by a boat. Then it happened.

You know how they always say that in your deepest, darkest moment, something will make you laugh? Well, that day I learned the old saying was true. As I stood there in my underwear, stuck in the mud with swamp creatures and muck oozing out of my every orifice, working harder than I've ever worked in my life, I looked up, caught a glimpse of my partner and burst out in laughter.

You see, he was Asian and at some point during this debacle, my pole-wielding partner had put on all of his anti-sun gear. I'd been so caught up with dislodging the boat, I hadn't paid much attention to him until that moment of desperation when I looked up and saw what looked like a masked, cloaked ninja on the back deck of my boat. And, if that wasn't funny enough, he made an unmistakable groan as he pushed, "Hiii-yaa, Hiiiiyeeeyah!"

After one of the longest, hardest laughs I've ever had, I finally came to the conclusion that not even I, the swamp monster, along with my partner, the ninja, were going to move this boat. Needless to say, we missed weigh-in, but we were ultimately saved by another boat with a very long tow rope.

TIP 126:
Don't Go Shakin' My Heart

One of the common mistakes with drop-shotting is overworking your bait. The whole reason this technique is a success is that the bait looks natural to fish. So make sure to keep it natural. Using a rod with a soft tip will allow you to slowly shake your bait without overworking it or moving the weight off the bottom. One thing a lot of anglers forget is that under the water there's current and movement. Without even moving a drop-shot rig, it's going to have some action. With this technique, less is definitely more.

TIP 127:
The Shape of Your Crank

When most people look at a box of cranks, all they see is different colours and baits that run at different depths. One thing to remember about cranks is they all have slightly different actions. Generally the rounder, fat-shaped baits have a wider wobble, while the slender more flat-shaped baits have a tighter wobble. This is key in crank selection. In dirty water I'll generally use a wider-wobbling bait that gives off more vibration, which makes it easier for the fish to find. In clear water it's easier for the fish to find the bait, so I'll use a flat-sided, tighter-wobbling bait that looks more natural.

TIP 128:
Map 'Em Out

I saw a bumper sticker once that said, "The secret to fishing is fish where the fish live." That sounds pretty simple, but how in the world do you find them? The simplest tip for this is to spend a little bit of time researching maps before you hit a lake. This will allow you to become more familiar with what's under the water. No matter what you're fishing for, once a year most fish spawn. We know where they do that — in the shallow back bays or rivers. The simplest and easiest approach to finding fish in an unfamiliar lake is to pick the most likely area they would have spawned in and follow the contours out from there. On the way out of their spawning areas, fish will stop on points, drop-offs, ledges and weed-lines. Once you find one area that is holding fish, use your map to find other areas that are similar and chances are you'll find more fish.

TIP 129:
Lower and Slower

Trolling motors probably weren't named properly, since very few people actually use them for trolling. It would have made a lot more sense to call them electric positioning motors. These motors allow you to manoeuvre your boat around the structure or cover that's holding the fish without having to use an anchor. However, one of the biggest mistakes anglers make with these motors is using them on too high a setting. It's a lot easier to control the boat if you place the motor on a lower setting, and you're less likely to spook fish when you're not thrashing around. Try running your trolling motor at a slower speed and see how your results change.

TIP 130:
Casting Lowdown

Casting can be a challenge, even on the calmest of days. But when the wind picks up, there's even more opportunity to screw up. One of the easiest ways to combat this is to keep your lure low to the water by casting sidearm. If you wind up and do a giant overhand long bomb, chances are the bait will get caught in the wind and blow back into your face. Not only that, you're more likely to get a nasty backlash.

TIP 131:
Move to the Dark Side

Some people say that to catch a fish, you have to think like a fish. Well, I don't want to do that. These things swim around in pee and crap where they live. But one time it pays to think like a fish is when it comes to night fishing. Generally, when people have to choose a bait for night fishing, they gravitate towards a bright-coloured lure. But you have to think about what a fish is seeing. When a fish looks up towards the surface under the moonlight, all it sees is a silhouette. A dark silhouette is a lot easier to pick up in those conditions than a light one. So when night fishing, leave the disco baits at home and tie on something dark.

TIP 132:
Set It Aside

Marker buoys are one of the tools I never hit the water without. When you find an area that's holding fish, you want to be able to stay on it and keep catching them. However, you quickly learn the smart move is to place your marker slightly off the spot. It's never good to drop a giant lead brick on top of the fish you're trying to catch. This trick will also keep other anglers from knowing exactly where you're fishing or what you're doing.

TIP 133:
Good Vibrations

When people explain why a fish hits their bait, they'll most likely tell you it's colour, scent or even size. One of the most important reasons for a fish striking, though, is vibration. A fish has what is known as a lateral line. This is just one of the things a fish has that we don't. Through the lateral line, the fish can feel vibration without touching the thing that's vibrating. This helps them feed at night and in dirty water conditions and is another reason why they don't bump into each other in the middle of a feeding frenzy. So how does this help you as an angler? Simple — pay attention to the action you can get out of your bait. Don't just reel your bait back to the boat — give it a quick pop or twitch every once in a while and you'll quickly learn that good vibrations is more than just a crappy Beach Boys song.

TIP 134:
Skipping

Some of the best fishing spots are the hardest to get your baits to, such as docks or overhanging trees. Sure, you can cast to the edge, but you know the big fish live way back under the cover where it's hard to reach. The easiest way to get back under these obstacles is by skipping your bait under the overhangs. The theory and principle in this is no different than what you did with flat-sided rocks as a kid. You want the bait to skip three to four times across the surface until it gets to the area.

With a low underarm cast, coupled with a lightly weighted bait, such as a tube, this can be easily accomplished. One of the best ways to learn this technique is to practise out in the open. Next time you're fishing a tube in the middle of the lake, try skipping it on the surface. True, there's no reason to do it out there, but the practice will give you confidence when you are faced with challenging cover.

TIP 135:
Go the Extra Distance

Crankbaits are amazingly effective lures. One thing to remember is that it takes a few cranks of the reel to get them to their desired depth. So, unlike other lures, a smart angler will actually cast past the piece of cover or structure they want to fish, so the crank has time to get to the proper depth by the time it reaches the money zone.

End of the Line

Some of you might be wondering how in the world I came up with all these tips. Well, I'd like to take credit and say I'm just that smart. But if you spend any time with me, you'll realize that isn't the case. Most of these tips are the results of an unrivalled list of disasters, muck-ups and downright dumb things I've done on the water. You name it, I've done it. Whether it's leaving the plug out of my boat, hooking myself or just simply forgetting my rods at home, I've done it all. (Hey, maybe I just came up with an idea for my next book.)

One thing I'm proud of, though, is that at least I learned from these things. It doesn't matter whether you host a fishing show like I do, compete in tournaments or are just trying to whup your brother's butt in the annual family fish-off — nobody likes to fail. Even worse than failing once is failing twice due to the same mistake. So, if I could guarantee that after reading this book you would never make some stupid mistake on the water, well, we probably would have charged you a lot more than what you paid for this book. But the coolest part about the sport of fishing is you never stop learning. So get out there, have fun and learn from your mistakes. With any luck, you won't make nearly as many as I did.

When fishing for slimy, smelly Alligator Gar in Texas, don't wear white.

Glossary

Abrasion Resistance: The ability of a fishing line not to get scuffed up. Lines with high abrasion resistance are generally stiffer, while lines with low abrasion resistance are limper.

Bail: The part of a spinning reel that is used to distribute the line on the spool. In order to cast, the bail is flipped open, whereas in order to retrieve, the bail is flipped closed. On some rods, the bail is flipped automatically by turning the reel crank.

Baitcasting/Casting Reel: The oldest form of mechanical fishing reel that incorporates a rotating spool. Original forms of this reel were direct drive, with the handle connected directly to the spool. These reels didn't offer very long casting distances due to the friction generated by rotating the spool and turning the gears and handle. On these older models, if an angler's fingers slipped off the handle while fighting a fish, the handle would reverse with force, which would result in the angler's knuckles getting damaged — hence their nickname, "Knuckle Buster."

Contemporary casting reels (that is, anything made since the sixties) all have free-floating spools that disengage the gears and handle for casting, which increases distance. These reels also use a drag system that allows a fish to pull line off the spool without the handle moving in the reverse direction.

Bell Sinker: A sinker or weight that resembles a bell. Through the centreline runs a wire, generally made of brass, that has a loop in one end where the angler ties the fishing line.

Bill: The part of a crankbait or jerkbait that causes the bait to dive and creates wobble. The bill is located at the front of the bait, under the line-tie.

Blade: A thin, cupped piece of metal or plastic that is attached to lures to provide flash and vibration. See Colorado Blade, Indiana Blade and Willow Leaf Blade.

Bobber: A float designed to suspend an angler's bait off the bottom of a river, lake or reservoir. Bobbers are attached to the angler's line above the lure and allow the angler to see when a fish takes the bait by sinking when the fish strikes and moves away. It's one of the few pieces of tackle an angler is happy to see disappear.

Bobber Stop/Stopper: A small latex rubber ball placed on an angler's line. Originally these were designed to be used with slip bobbers so an angler could place a bait or lure at a specific depth. They have found many other uses in fishing, though, such as for pegging a sliding sinker or as a shock absorber between a slip sinker and knot.

Bottom-Contact Bait: Any bait that is worked on the bottom of a lake, reservoir or river.

Braided Line: Line manufactured by braiding multiple smaller line filaments together. Also known as super-line.

Carolina Rig: A method of presenting a soft plastic lure, like a worm or grub, using a sliding egg sinker placed on the main line and a swivel attached below the sinker. A leader, anywhere from two to six feet in length, is attached to the other end of the swivel and a hook attached to the end of the leader. This technique allows a fish to pick up the bait but not feel the resistance of the sinker since the line can freely run through it. The Carolina rig can also be used to present live bait. Also known as a North Carolina rig or C-rig.

Casting Gear: A rod and reel setup that uses a casting reel.

Colorado Blade: This nearly circular style of blade puts out the most vibration and flash of all the blade styles.

Crankbait: In general terms, a crankbait is any hard plastic or wood bait that resembles a baitfish or crawdad and is used by casting and retrieving at a steady pace. In more specific terms, this genre of baits includes only those lures that are short and fat and have a diving bill.

Craw: Abbreviated term for crawdad or crayfish.

Downrigger Release Clip: A clip that releases an angler's line from the downrigger ball. The downrigger ball is not a fancy party for anglers, and if it were I would not want to be released from it anyway.

Drop-Shotting: A technique used to present a bait or soft plastic lure off the bottom. A drop-shot rig, also known as a down-shot rig, is tied with the sinker at the end of the line and the hook above the sinker.

Egg Sinker: Shaped like an egg, this sinker has a hole through the centreline that the line runs through.

Feathered Treble Hook: A triple hook that has been dressed with feathers to add more action or bulk to a lure.

Feathering the Line: A technique used in casting in which the angler applies slight pressure to either the spool of a casting reel or the line as it comes off a spinning reel in order to control the distance of a cast.

Grub: A short, fat plastic lure used to imitate a small baitfish or crawdad.

Herring Dodger: A string of blades rigged in front of a leader and used to attract fish from a long distance. A herring dodger is used while trolling.

Hook: A device that represents about the biggest mistake a fish can ever make, but which provides anglers with great pleasure. *See also* Stock Hook, Trailer Hook, Treble Hook.

Hookset: The action of jerking the fishing rod hard in order to drive the hook into a fish's mouth.

Indiana Blade: A style of blade shaped like a teardrop. Since this blade style has less surface area, it puts out less vibration and flash than a Colorado blade.

Insert Rattle: A rattle made to be inserted into a lure. It is usually made from glass but plastic insert rattles are also available.

Jerkbait: Long, slender lures that imitate a minnow, made from either plastic or wood. Anglers make them seem more natural by jerking the bait through the water in order to imitate a minnow—thus the nickname jerkbait.

Jig: A lure that incorporates a weighted hook (leadhead), a skirt and a trailer. The skirt can be made of either soft plastic or strands of silicon, and the trailer can be either a soft plastic or a piece of cured pork rind. The lure can be worked slowly on the bottom to imitate a crawdad or retrieved fast to imitate a baitfish.

Jighead: A hook with a cast lead or tungsten weight at or near the eye of the hook. Leadheads come in a range of weights and a dizzying number of styles, including ball heads, football heads, Arky heads, Aspirin heads and tube heads, with each style having a specific use.

Jumpy Drag: It doesn't sound like fun, and it's not. A jumpy drag does not allow line to come off the reel spool smoothly and can lead to lost fish, since the jerking effect of a jumpy drag can loosen a hook in a fish's mouth. Now that is a drag. To solve this problem, have the reel serviced by changing out the drag washers.

Keeper Barb: A small barb on the shank of a hook designed to hold a bait or soft plastic lure at that location on the hook.

Leader: A length of line that is placed below a swivel on a Carolina rig. The hook is attached at the end of this line.

Leadhead: See Jighead.

Levelwind: The line-distribution mechanism on a casting reel that arranges the line evenly on the spool.

Light-Wire Hook: A hook made with fine diameter wire. Generally used when fishing light lines.

Lure: An artificial bait used to coax a fish into thinking it's something good to eat, when in fact it's about the worst possible thing a fish could put in its mouth.

Lure Wrap: A wrap placed around a lure in order to keep its hooks from tangling other objects nearby, like other lures, an angler's clothes or even his fingers.

Pegging a Sinker: Fixing a sliding sinker, like a worm weight or egg sinker, on the line. The phrase comes from the time when a toothpick was jammed in the hole of these sinkers to prevent them from sliding along the line. Today, toothpicks have been replaced by bobber stops, since a toothpick can harm the line.

Rattle Bait: A generic term used to describe a vibration bait like a Rattle Trap, Rattlin' Vibe or any other trap-style lure.

Rig: A specific way to use a lure, like a Carolina rig, a Texas rig, a drop-shot rig and many others.

Rod Guides: The circular appendages placed on a rod that guide the line up and down its length. They are commonly called "eyes."

Rod Sock: A tube of fabric or other soft material that is placed over a rod in order to protect it from damage.

Rubbercore Sinker: A long cylindrically-shaped sinker that has a groove down the centreline. Within the groove is placed a core of rubber used to attach the line.

Rubber O-Ring: Generally used as a seal in many mechanical pieces of equipment, rubber O-rings have found their way into the tackle boxes of anglers as a good method to save money while using a wacky rig. Because the hook is run under the O-ring, instead of through the soft plastic of the lure, the lure will last longer.

Senko: A soft stickbait (worm) invented by Gary Yamamoto Custom Baits. Although most soft-plastic manufacturers now make this style bait and call them by many names, the genre of bait is best known as the Senko.

Shrink Tubing: Used to seal wire connectors and in other electronics applications, shrink tubing has been found to be a great material to make custom keeper barbs on hooks.

Sinker: Another name for a weight, a sinker is used to "sink" a lure or bait.

Sliding Sinker: A type of sinker that slides on the line. Also called a slip sinker. *See* Worm Weight.

Snag: An object, like a tree, dock or weeds, that catches a lure. Otherwise known as a "pain in the neck."

Spinnerbait: A type of lure that incorporates a leadhead jig and a wire assembly with blades. On the leadhead portion of the bait is a skirt. This lure is used to mimic a baitfish.

Spinning Reel: A reel with a fixed spool on which line is distributed by a rotating bail.

Split Ring: A connector used between a lure and the line that allows the lure to have more action while being retrieved. A split ring is the same as the ring used on a keychain, only much smaller, and can either be round or oval in shape.

Split Shot: A small, spherical type of sinker that is crimped onto the line with pliers. These little sinkers resemble shot used in shotgun shells, though they have a slot either moulded or cut into them.

Split-Shot Rig: A technique to rig a soft plastic lure with a split-shot sinker. The split-shot rig is a finesse rig used when the fishing is tough.

Spool Tension Knob: A knob, located on the sideplate of a reel, that applies pressure on the reel's spool shaft. It's used to adjust spool tension so an angler can cast farther or decrease the opportunity for a backlash.

Staging: Fish will move around in stages, pausing in one place before moving on to another. This pause in the fish's cycle is called staging. For example, salmon stage in pools before heading up riffles, and bass will stage off ledges prior to moving onto flats to spawn.

Star Drag: Located underneath the handle of the reel, the star drag is used to either tighten or loosen the reel's drag system.

Stock Hook: A hook taken right out of the box — that is, before being sharpened or manipulated in other ways. You probably know someone who's not satisfied with the stock exhaust on his truck or feels the stock carburetors on his motorcycle could be improved with some tinkering and a pile of money (perhaps that's you). Well, anglers are no different with their hooks or other parts of their tackle.

Sweep: A type of hooksetting in which an angler sweeps the rod to the side instead of straight up.

Swimbait: A term that originally described a very large lure used in California to mimic a trout. These lures were as much as 12 inches long. Now the term generically describes any lure, 4 to 16 inches in length, designed to mimic a baitfish. The lure is cast out and brought back to the boat with a steady "swimming" retrieve.

Swivel: A piece of tackle that can be used on the line between the reel and the lure to help eliminate line twist.

Tag End: The end piece of line that's created when tying a knot.

Texas Rig: A technique for getting soft plastic baits through the weeds. This rig uses a worm weight that slides down to the head of the bait on the hook. The hook is placed in the soft plastic lure so as to be weedless.

Topwater Bait: A lure that is worked on the surface of the water.

Trailer: A lure added to a jig or spinnerbait for added action or bulk, or to make the bait more lifelike. Many lures, like grubs or plastic crawdads, can be used as trailers.

Trailer Hook: A second hook placed on the main hook of a spinnerbait to help catch fish that strike short.

Treble Hook: A hook with three points.

Trolling Motor: Also known as an electric motor, a trolling motor is used mainly to position a boat without making much noise.

Tube Bait: A hollow soft plastic lure with cut tentacles on one end. The bait was invented by Bobby and Gary Garland and originally called a Gitzit. Now the term tube bait encompasses this genre of lures.

Underarm Roll Cast: A method of casting in which the angler rotates their wrist backwards during a cast, thus rolling the tip of the rod underhand, creating a trajectory that is close to the water. This method of casting is great for short accurate casts or when casting in stiff winds.

Wacky Rig: A technique in which a worm is rigged by hooking it through the centre of the bait. Needless to say, a wacky worm is a worm rigged this way.

Weight Peg: See Bobber Stop/Stopper.

Willow Leaf Blade: A style of blade used on a number of lures to provide vibration and flash. This blade style is thinner than the Colorado and Indiana styles and is used under high fishing pressure conditions when the fish have seen a lot of other baits and you want to show them something different, or when less flash and vibration are desired.

Wind Knot: Also called a loose line, a wind knot is a loose loop of line that materializes on spinning reels when the angler does not ensure the line is tight on the spool after closing the bail.

Worm Harness: A leader generally made with two hooks snelled to the line and used for rigging a live worm.

Worm Weight: A conical weight designed for Texas-rigging a soft plastic worm, grub or other soft plastic lure.

Acknowledgements

I would like to dedicate my first book (notice I said *first* book—now that is positive thinking!) to my amazing wife and children, and to my whole family, especially my mom and dad, who took me fishing. Without those early childhood fishing trips, I would most likely be a broke stand-up comic appearing at every tiny bowling alley and senior citizens home across the country!

Thank you to my loyal fans for your support over the years. Please don't stop supporting me. And if you haven't already, buy my book! Even better, buy one for all your friends.

APR - - 2013